PATTERN HATCHING

Design Patterns Applied

The Software Patterns Series

Series Editor: John M. Vlissides

The Software Patterns Series (SPS) comprises pattern literature of lasting significance to software developers. Software patterns document general solutions to recurring problems in all software-related spheres, from the technology itself, to the organizations that develop and distribute it, to the people who use it. Books in the series distill experience from one or more of these areas into a form that software professionals can apply immediately. *Relevance* and *impact* are the tenets of the SPS. Relevance means each book presents patterns that solve real problems. Patterns worthy of the name are intrinsically relevant; they are borne of practitioners' experiences, not theory or speculation. Patterns have impact when they change how people work for the better. A book becomes a part of the series not just because it embraces these tenets, but because it has demonstrated it fulfills them for its audience.

Titles in the series:

The Design Patterns Smalltalk Companion, Sherman Alpert/Kyle Brown/Bobby Woolf

Pattern Languages of Program Design 3, edited by Robert Martin/Dirk Riehle/Frank Buschmann

Pattern Hatching: Design Patterns Applied, John Vlissides

Please see our web site at http://www.awl.com/cseng/swpatterns
for more information on these titles.

PATTERN HATCHING
Design Patterns Applied

John Vlissides
IBM T.J. Watson Research

ADDISON-WESLEY
An imprint of Addison Wesley Longman, Inc.

Reading, Massachusetts • Harlow, England • Menlo Park, California
Berkeley, California • Don Mills, Ontario • Sydney
Bonn • Amsterdam • Tokyo • Mexico City

Many of the designations used by manufacturers and sellers to distinguish their products are claimed as trademarks. Where those designations appear in this book and Addison-Wesley was aware of a trademark claim, the designations have been printed in initial caps or all caps.

The author and publisher have taken care in the preparation of this book, but make no expressed or implied warranty of any kind and assume no responsibility for errors or omissions. No liability is assumed for incidental or consequential damages in connection with or arising out of the use of the information or programs contained herein.

The publisher offers discounts on this book when ordered in quantity for special sales. For more information, please contact:

Corporate, Government, and Special Sales Group
Addison Wesley Longman, Inc.
One Jacob Way
Reading, Massachusetts 01867

Library of Congress Cataloging-in-Publication Data

Vlissides, John.
    Pattern hatching : design patterns applied   /   John Vlissides.
            p.   cm. — (Software patterns series)
    Includes bibliographical references and index.
    ISBN 0-201-43293-5 (alk. paper)
        1. Computer software—Development.   I. Title.   II. Series.
QA.76.D47V86   1998
005.1'2--dc21   98-20524
                                                                    CIP

Text printed on recycled and acid-free paper.

1 2 3 4 5 6 7 8 9 10 – MA – 02 01 00 99 98
First printing, June 1998

Contents

Foreword

John filled a void in my life when he wrote and told me about his plans to write a pattern column for *C++ Report*. In particular, he filled about five voids a year—I was writing a column on patterns that appeared every other month, and Stan Lippman suggested that John alternate with me. John was going to focus on design patterns in particular, while I kept the broader focus of my column. I was thrilled to become part of a duo that would take patterns to the C++ community, and I liked John's approach to the topic. I wrote him that:

> The hatching analogy is cute—and makes a very good point. I just went back and read the Preface to the second edition of Alexander's *Notes on Synthesis*, and he's clearly into the discovery of things that lurk in nature waiting to be revealed, rather than focusing on "methods" to create them or even to pry them from their jeweled crevasses.

It was not only a pleasure, but an honor, to share the space with one of the Gang of Four (GoF) authors. You probably would never have heard of patterns had it not been for the GoF's *Design Patterns* book; the GoF book served the pattern discipline well by getting the word out. The GoF's design patterns established a humble but noble foundation that broadened into the pattern community we know today. And this book offers first-hand insights into the thought processes of one of the GoF authors, as well as second-hand insights into the broader process.

You have to break a few eggs to make a good pattern, and John's columns explore egg-breaking dialogue that must have taken place behind the scenes in the making of the GoF book. For example, John explores the limitations of VISITOR in the context of an evolving class structure. He talks about patterns, like GENERATION GAP, that didn't make it into the GoF book but that were probably good enough to be published anyhow (GENERATION GAP appears here in Chapter 3, Themes and Variations). You can find the GoF's dialogue about the MULTICAST pattern, which caused John to reflect: "Those who ascribe extraordinary powers to the Gang of Four will be appalled by our generally chaotic process of pattern development." This book conveys something very important that's missing in the more academic and polished *Design Patterns* book—that patterns are the result of real, working programmers who don't get everything right the first time, and who struggle with the pragmatics of recurring design practices. I think pattern users who read this book will better appreciate the effort that went into the GoF patterns, and I think pattern writers who read this book will approach pattern mining and pattern writing with heightened humility and diligence than before.

Ordre ex chaos is a theme in the natural sciences, and we shouldn't expect the science of design to be any different. Patterns are about people working together to discover and document constructs that contribute to the quality of life of humanity as a whole. It is a necessarily organic process. Through this book, you'll gain insights into the organic process behind those patterns, the thought processes of ordinary (but very experienced and dutiful) software developers struggling with their own understanding of design. The *Design Patterns* book is one distillation of their collective understanding. *Pattern Hatching* is a distillation of the process that generated that understanding, and its value in interpreting the GoF shouldn't be underestimated. Let me relate some mail I got from Richard Helm in late 1997 that I believe corroborates this point:

> GoF design patterns address only aspects of micro-architecture. You also have to get the macro-architecture right: layering, distribution, functional isolation, . . . ; and the nano-architecture right as Cope says: encapsulation, Liskov. . . . And somewhere in all of that a pattern might

just be used, but maybe not, and probably quite unlike it has been written, described in some book.

This book will help you understand how the GoF book—and, indeed, any collection of design patterns—can be a treasured guide without being a burdensome prescription. It helps place design patterns in their rightful place in the broader context of basic object-oriented design principles. It brings out the informal yet intense criteria and iterative process that led to the 23 patterns between the *Design Patterns* covers. It's liberating to know that such a process took place, and to know how it took place, because it brings the patterns down to earth where pragmatic day-to-day considerations rule. I think that will help the reader understand the importance of tailoring patterns to the problem at hand; it will help the reader engage his or her own intellect instead of *blindly* following a formalism "described in some book." I don't think computer scientists will like this book, but real programmers will ponder it, identify with it, and greatly appreciate it.

James O. Coplien
Lucent Technologies
Bell Labs Innovations

Preface

I'll never forget how I felt one autumn afternoon back in 1994. I had just received an e-mail message from Stan Lippman, then-editor-in-chief of C++ *Report*, extending me an offer to write a bimonthly column for that magazine.

We were the merest acquaintances, having met earlier in the year when he toured the Watson Lab. We had chatted briefly about his work on development tools and about the GoF's work on patterns. Unlike most people at the time, Stan was familiar with the pattern concept—he had read successive preprints of *Design Patterns* and had encouraging things to say about it. Be that as it may, the conversation drifted quickly toward the art of writing in general; and as it did, I remember feeling increasingly pretentious, like I was out of my league. Here was Stan, noted columnist and author of two highly successful books, discussing his craft with a rank amateur. I wasn't sure if he was enjoying our conversation or just tolerating it until his next appointment. (I've since learned that Stan's tolerance is surpassed only by his sincerity!)

Yet those feelings of inadequacy were nothing compared to my reaction to his e-mail a few months later. I experienced a strange combination of elation and terror at the prospect of writing regularly for an international audience. Could I keep it up for more than a couple of installments? Would people care what I had to say? What *did* I have to say? And if I said it, would it help anyone?

I indulged my fears for nearly an hour. Then some of my Dad's admonitions started coming back to me: Self-consciousness breeds paralysis, I was told, not in so many words. Focus on the fundamentals, and everything else will follow. "Just do it," he had said, well before Nike would.

So I did.

Choosing a theme was easy enough. By that point I had been knee-deep in pattern research for nearly three years. We had recently completed the *Design Patterns* book, but we all knew it was far from the final word on the topic. A column would be a great forum for expounding on that material, for extending it, and for addressing new issues as they arose. It didn't hurt that a column could help sales too—if it did the book justice.

Now, after more than a dozen installments of my "Pattern Hatching" column, I think it's safe to say my fears were unfounded. I'm never at a loss for something to write, and I always have fun writing it. I've also received lots of encouraging feedback from people worldwide, including recurring solicitations for old installments. After a while that got me to thinking about a one-stop shop for my columns, along with any other pattern stuff I had that was useful and had gone unpublished.

This book is meant to fill that bill. In it you'll find thoughts and ideas from the first three years of my column-writing career, including everything I've published in *C++ Report* and *Object Magazine*, plus a smattering of new insights. I've arranged it in logical order rather than temporally so that it reads as a book should. That was easier than it might have been, because many of the articles were part of this or that series, but it still took some doing. I hope you enjoy the result.

Acknowledgments

As always, there are many people to thank for multifarious assistance. First and foremost are my fellow Gang of Four members—Erich Gamma, Richard Helm, and Ralph Johnson. Each one offered valuable feedback at one point or another, the sum of which made this a much different (and certainly better) book. It's a rare privilege to work with people who so complement one another, and I'm very grateful for it.

They weren't unrivaled in their help, however. Several others took time to plow through rough drafts in search of non sequiturs, faux pas, and the all-too-familiar *lapsus calami*. These indomitable souls include Bruce Anderson, Bard Bloom, Frank Buschmann, Jim Coplien, Rey Crisostomo, Wim De Pauw, Kirk Knoernschild, John Lakos, Doug Lea, Bob Martin, Dirk Riehle, Doug Schmidt, and Peri Tarr. An added word of thanks goes to Jim, my alter ego in the *Report*, for his gracious Foreword to this book and just for being an all-around inspiring guy.

Next come the total strangers who have e-written me questions, comments, corrections, and good-natured chides. There are many in this category, but I'll list only those whom I have quoted or whose comments were relevant to this volume: Mark Betz, Laurion Burchall, Chris Clark, Richard Gyger, Michael Hittesdorf, Michael McCosker, Scott Meyers, Tim Peierls, Paul Pelletier, Ranjiv Sharma, David Van Camp, Gerolf Wendland, and Barbara Zino. And even though I haven't identified the rest of you, please realize that I'm no less obliged for your input.

Finally, I thank two families, one natural, the other professional, for supporting me in untold ways. I owe both a great debt.

Hawthorne, New York
January 1998

J.V.
vlis@watson.ibm.com

PATTERN HATCHING

Design Patterns Applied

CHAPTER 1 — *Introduction*

If you've never heard of a book called *Design Patterns: Elements of Reusable Object-Oriented Software* [GoF95], now would be an excellent time to obtain a copy before reading further here. Ditto if you've heard of that book and perhaps even own a copy but have never really *studied* it.

If you're still with me, I'll assume you fall into neither of those categories. That means you know a bit about patterns in general and about our set of 23 design patterns in particular. You'll need that much to benefit from *Pattern Hatching*, because it extends, updates, and otherwise enhances the material in *Design Patterns*. The insights here will be largely inaccessible to you if you're unfamiliar with the so-called *Gang of Four*, or *GoF*, patterns—the aforementioned 23. In fact, it would be good to have *Design Patterns* handy as you read this book. I also assume you're facile with C++, which should be reasonable given we make the same assumption in *Design Patterns*.

Now, I hope you'll forgive me for this, but just as a reality check, see if you can state the intent of the COMPOSITE pattern in 25 words or less. You might want to turn away for a minute to think about it.

1

Did the intent roll off your tongue word-for-word? If yes, you'll have no trouble here. In fact, you're probably *too* serious about this stuff. Consider taking up a hobby or two. If you knew the intent but just had trouble putting it into words, don't worry—this book is for you too.

If, however, you drew a complete blank, my opening paragraph has failed us miserably. I suggest you put this book down, pick up a copy of *Design Patterns*, turn to page 163, and read through to the end of the Implementation section. Do the same for the other patterns listed on page *xv* of that book. That exercise should give you enough background to make this book worth your while.

Why "Pattern Hatching," you wonder? I chose that title initially for its similarity to a familiar concept in computer science. (Besides, all the good pattern titles were taken.) But I've since come around to thinking that it captures my intent for this material rather well. *Hatching* doesn't suggest we are creating anything; it implies development from preexisting rudiments. And that happens to be appropriate: *Design Patterns* is our carton of eggs, as it were, from which hopefully much new life will emerge.[1]

Be assured I'm not merely echoing *Design Patterns* here. My aim is to build on it, to leverage its concepts and make them that much more useful to you. You will discover techniques for applying certain patterns and not applying others, as circumstances dictate. You will encounter new insights on some of our original patterns, and you will witness the process by which we develop new patterns. There are lots of examples too. Some are time-tested designs; others are experimental, which is a nice way of saying "half-baked." Still others are entirely speculative—unabashed paper designs that would probably wither in reality's harsh light, but they may also contain the seeds of more robust designs.

I'm exposing you to this stuff with a sincere desire that your design sensibilities will deepen, your pattern awareness will heighten, and your outlook on software development will broaden. These have been my experiences using patterns. I hope they become your own.

---

1. I trust we won't have occasion to take this analogy too much further.

The Top Ten Misconceptions

Along with all the hoopla surrounding patterns these days comes more than a little confusion, consternation, and misinformation. This is partly a reflection of how new the field is to mainstream software developers even though it's not, strictly speaking, a new field. It's a fast-moving field too, creating vacuums of facts. And yes, we pattern proponents deserve some of the blame for not educating people as thoroughly as we'd like, though not for lack of trying [BMR+96, Coplien96, CS95, GoF95, MRB98, VCK96].

So I feel duty-bound to redress the more glaring misconceptions about patterns—misconceptions I've heard often enough to qualify them as patterns in their own right. I even toyed with using a pattern form to articulate them . . . until it dawned on me that reducing everything to patterns was itself a misconception! Anyway, please remember that I'm not speaking for the pattern community. I expect most pattern cognoscenti would agree these are prevalent misconceptions, but they may disagree with how I dispel them.

Having mulled over the things I've heard people say about patterns through the years, it seems the misconceptions fall into three categories: misconceptions about what patterns *are*, misconceptions about what they *can do*, and misconceptions about the community that's been promoting them. Each of my "top ten" falls into one of these categories. So I'll organize them accordingly, looking first at misconceptions about what patterns *are*.

Misconception 1:
"A pattern is a solution to a problem in a context."

This definition was inspired by Christopher Alexander [AIS+77], so calling it a misconception may seem like heresy to some. But this simple counterexample should make its deficiency clear:

Problem: How do I redeem my winning lottery ticket before it expires?

Context: The dog ate the ticket an hour before the deadline.

Solution: Cut the dog open, fish out the ticket, and run to the nearest redemption station.

This is a solution to a problem in a context. It is not a pattern. What's missing? At least three things:

1. *Recurrence*, which makes the solution relevant in situations outside the immediate one.

2. *Teaching*, which gives you the understanding to tailor the solution to a variant of the problem. (Most of the teaching in real patterns lies in the description and resolution of forces, and/or the consequences of application.)

3. A *name* by which to refer to the pattern.

To be sure, a satisfactory definition has proven elusive, as witnessed by the ongoing debate within the "pattern-discussion" mailing list, *patterns-discussion@cs.uiuc.edu*.[2] Contributing to the difficulty is the fact that a pattern is both a thing and a description of similar things. One way to differentiate the two is to use the term *pattern* consistently to refer to the description and use *pattern instance* to refer to a concrete application of a pattern.

But defining terms may prove a futile exercise anyway, because a definition that's meaningful to one audience (say, programmers) might be totally meaningless to another (say, executives holding the purse strings). I certainly won't try to come up with the ultimate definition here. Suffice it to say, any definition that stipulates a pattern's constituent parts must talk about recurrence, teaching, and naming in addition to problem, solution, and context.

Misconception 2:
"Patterns are just jargon, rules, programming tricks, data structures. . . ."

I call this "the belittling dismissal." It's natural to try to reduce something unfamiliar to something known, especially if you're not particularly motivated to investigate the unfamiliar. Plus, all too often, people put old wine in new skins and call it innovation. It's good to be wary.

Yet the belittling dismissal does not come from experience. Often it's based on superficial familiarity, with an added dash of cynicism. Besides, nothing is ever totally new; people have had patterns in their heads for as long as there have been heads. What's new is that we've started naming the patterns and writing them down.

---

2. To subscribe, send e-mail with the lone word "subscribe" as its subject (and no quotes!) to *patterns-discussion-request@cs.uiuc.edu*.

About those comparisons: There is, in fact, a pattern jargon—terms such as "pattern" itself, "forces," Alexander's "quality without a name," and so forth. But patterns hardly reduce to jargon. Compared to most areas of computer science, patterns introduce few new terms. That's symptomatic, actually. A good pattern is inherently accessible to its audience. It may well use the jargon of its target domain, but there's rarely a need for pattern-specific terminology.

Neither are patterns rules you can apply mindlessly (the teaching component works against that) nor are they limited to programming tricks, even though the "idioms" branch of the discipline focuses on patterns that are programming language-specific. "Tricks" is a tad pejorative to my ear as well, and it overemphasizes solution at the expense of problem, context, teaching, and naming.

No doubt you've heard of an innovation's three stages of acceptance: First it's dismissed as rubbish, then it's merely nonviable, and finally it's obvious and trivial—"What we've done all along." Patterns aren't entirely out of stage one yet.

Misconception 3:
"Seen one, seen them all."

Broad-brushing is unfair as a rule, and that goes double for pattern broad-brushing. There's a bewildering range of pattern domains, content, scope, styles, and quality—just flip through one of the *Pattern Languages of Program Design* books [CS95, MRB98, VCK96] and you'll see. Patterns are as diverse as the people who write them, perhaps more so; authors like Alistair Cockburn, Jim Coplien, Neil Harrison, and Ralph Johnson (to name a few) have gone beyond their initial forays to write patterns of varied styles and domains. It would be a mistake to draw sweeping conclusions about patterns from just a few examples.

Misconception 4:
"Patterns need tool or methodological support to be effective."

Having written, used, and helped others use patterns over the past five years, and having helped perpetrate at least one pattern-based tool [BFV+96], I can state confidently that the benefit from patterns comes mostly from applying them as they are—that is, with no support of any kind.

When I speak on this topic, I usually point out four main benefits of patterns:

1. They capture expertise and make it accessible to nonexperts.
2. Their names collectively form a vocabulary that helps developers communicate better.
3. They help people understand a system more quickly when it is documented with the patterns it uses.
4. They facilitate restructuring a system whether or not it was designed with patterns in mind.

For the longest time I thought item 1 provided the bulk of the benefit. Now I realize that benefit 2 is at least as important. Think about it: How many bytes of information flow between developers, either verbally or electronically, in the course of a development project? My guess is megabytes if not gigabytes. (I collected several dozen megabytes of e-mail that circulated among the Gang of Four as we wrote *Design Patterns*. I'd say our effort approximates that of a small-to-medium-sized software development project.) With so much communication going on, anything that makes it incrementally more efficient would yield substantial time savings. Patterns thus expand people's communication bandwidth. My appreciation of benefits 3 and 4 is growing too, especially as projects get ever-larger and their software longer-lived.

In short, patterns are primarily food for the brain, not fodder for a tool. There may yet be latent benefit in methodological or automated support, but I'm convinced it'll be icing on the cake, not the cake itself or even a layer thereof.

The misconceptions I've looked at so far have to do with what patterns *are*. Now for a few misconceptions about what patterns *can do*. These come in two flavors: the overstating kind and the understating kind.

Misconception 5:
"Patterns guarantee reusable software, higher productivity, world peace, etc."

This one's easy, because *patterns don't guarantee anything*. They don't even make benefit *likely*. Patterns do nothing to remove the human from the creative process. They merely bring hope of empowerment to a possibly inexperienced, perhaps just uninitiated, but otherwise capable and creative person.

People speak of good patterns producing an "Aha!" response. That can only occur if the pattern strikes a chord in the reader's mind. If it doesn't, then the pattern is like the proverbial tree that falls in the forest with no one around to hear it—did it make a sound? So too with patterns: What good is a pattern, no matter how well-written, if it doesn't produce a resonance in the human mind?

Patterns are just another weapon in the developer's arsenal. To ascribe much more to them is counterproductive. Underpromise and overdeliver—that's the best defense against hype and backlash.

Misconception 6:
"Patterns 'generate' whole architectures."

This misconception is like unto the last one, only it's less aggressive in its overstatement.

The generative aspect of patterns gets discussed periodically in the pattern forums. As I understand it, *generativity* refers to a pattern's ability to create *emergent behavior*. That's a fancy way of saying the pattern helps the reader solve problems that the pattern doesn't address explicitly. Some of what I've read suggests that true generativity makes this happen almost in spite of one's self.

To me, the key to generativity is in the parts of a pattern dedicated to teaching—the forces and their resolution, for example, or the discussion of consequences. These insights are particularly useful as you define and refine an architecture. But patterns themselves don't generate anything—people do, and they do it only if both they and the patterns they use are up to snuff. Moreover, patterns are unlikely to cover every aspect of an architecture. Show me a nontrivial design, and I'll show you lots of design issues that no pattern addresses. Perhaps they are not common or recurring issues, or if they are, they have yet to be written up in pattern form. In any event, it's up to you to fill the whitespace between patterns with your own creativity.

Misconception 7:
"Patterns are for (object-oriented) design or implementation."

At the other end of the spectrum are unduly limiting misconceptions like this one. Frankly I'm surprised anyone would believe it, and yet enough people have asked me about it to earn this misconception a place in the top ten. If it seems overly naive to you, skip to the next misconception.

Patterns are nothing if they don't capture expertise. The nature of that expertise is left open to the pattern writer. Certainly there's expertise worth capturing in object-oriented software design, but there's just as much to be had in non-object-oriented design—and not just design but analysis, maintenance, testing, documentation, organizational structure, and on and on. Patterns in these varied areas are now emerging. Already there are at least two books on analysis patterns [Fowler97, Hay96], and each Pattern Languages of Programs (PLoP) conference attracts new kinds of patterns. (A particularly interesting submission to the 1996 conference concerned patterns for music composition!)

Like most misconceptions, there's a grain of truth in this one. When you look at the pattern forms people use, you see variations on two basic styles: the highly structured GoF style used in *Design Patterns* and the near-belletristic style of Christopher Alexander—narrative, with minimal structure. Having dabbled in pattern writing for something other than object-oriented design, I now recognize how biased the GoF style is toward its domain. It just plain doesn't work for other areas of expertise I've tried. What should the Structure diagram look like for a C++ idiom? The implementation trade-offs in a pattern for music composition? The Collaborations in a pattern for good expository writing?

Clearly, one pattern format does not fit all. What does fit all is the general concept of pattern as a vehicle for capturing and conveying expertise, whatever the field.

Misconception 8:
"There's no evidence that patterns help anybody."

This one held water in the past, but not anymore. People are reporting benefits from patterns in journals such as *Software—Practice and Experience* [Kotula96], and conferences such as OOPSLA [HJE95, Schmid95] and ICSE [BCC+96]. Doug Schmidt has articulated several benefits in the context of teaching computer science to undergraduates and graduates [PD96]. Although most of this evidence is qualitative, I know of at least one group that is conducting controlled experiments in an attempt at more quantitative results [Prechelt97, PUS97].

As time progresses, we'll get a better handle on the benefits and pitfalls of pattern usage. Even though initial returns are promising, we need more experience for a thorough assessment. But it would be foolish indeed to reject patterns out of hand just because their benefits aren't fully quantified.

So much for fallacies about what patterns can do. The last two misconceptions concern not patterns per se but the community that has championed them.

Misconception 9:
"The pattern community is a clique of elites."

I'd love to know how these notions get started, because if there's one noteworthy aspect of the pattern community, it is its diversity. This is easily gauged from the attendees of the PLoP conferences—people from all over the world, from large corporations and small start-ups; analysts, designers, and implementors; students and professors; big-name authors and fledglings. I was surprised to learn that more than one regular attendee isn't even a computer scientist! The community is still in flux too, with ample turnover in attendees from year to year.

Given the pattern community's penchant for publishing, one might wonder at the relative scarcity of academics. The fact is that most PLoP attendees are practitioners. It seems to have always been so. Not one of the prominent early proponents of software patterns—including Kent Beck, Peter Coad, and Ward Cunningham—comes from an academic background. Only one of the Gang of Four (Ralph) is from academia, and he's the most applied academic I know. The grassroots nature of the pattern community is clearly at odds with any insinuation of homogeneity and elitism.

Misconception 10:
"The pattern community is self-serving, even conspiratorial."

More than once I've heard the charge that patterns' primary use is as a source of revenue for those who write books about them. It has even been suggested that the patterns "movement" has a nefarious agenda.

Poppycock!

Speaking as one of the Gang of Four, I can affirm that we were as surprised as anyone by the reaction to *Design Patterns*. Certainly none of us was ready for the feeding frenzy at its OOPSLA '94 debut—even the publisher was caught off-guard by the demand. Throughout the project our overriding concern was to create the highest-quality book we could. We were too busy just trying to understand this stuff to be distracted by sales issues.

That was then. Now that *pattern* has achieved buzzword status, it's inevitable that some will leverage the term for less than altruistic purposes. But if you read the works of leading pattern authors carefully, you'll sense a common and overarching desire: to take hard-earned expertise, best practices, even competitive advantage—the fruits of years of hands-on experience—and not just disclose it but *impart* it to all comers.

It is this passion for improving the reader's lot that motivates a sincere and effective pattern author. Anything less is self-defeating—and the ultimate misconception about patterns.

Observations

Once past the fallacies, people tend to react to design patterns in one of two ways. I'll try to describe them by way of analogy.

Picture an electronics hobbyist who, though bereft of formal training, has nevertheless designed and built a slew of useful gadgets over the years: a ham radio, a geiger counter, a security alarm, and many others. One day the hobbyist decides it's time to get some official recognition for this talent by going back to school and earning a degree in electronics. As the coursework unfolds, the hobbyist is struck by how familiar the material seems. It's not the terminology or the presentation that's familiar but the underlying concepts. The hobbyist keeps seeing names and rationalizations for stuff he's used implicitly for years. It's just one epiphany after another.

Cut now to the freshman taking the same classes and studying the same material. He has no electronics background—lots of roller-blading, yes, but no electronics. The stuff in the course is intensely painful for him, not because he's dumb, but because it's so totally new. It takes quite a bit more time for the freshman to understand and appreciate the material. But eventually he does, with hard work and a bit of perseverance.

If you feel like a design pattern hobbyist, then more power to you. If, on the other hand, you feel more like a freshman, take heart: The investment you make learning good patterns will pay for itself each time you apply them in your designs. That's a promise.

But maybe electronics, with its "techie" connotations, isn't the best analogy for everyone. If you agree, then consider something Alfred North Whitehead said in 1943, admittedly in a different context, that might nonetheless make a more appealing connection:

> Art is the imposing of a pattern on experience, and our aesthetic enjoyment in recognition of the pattern.

CHAPTER 2

Designing with Patterns

The best way to get a feel for using patterns is, well, to *just use* them. The challenge for yours truly is coming up with an example everyone can appreciate. People are most interested in their own problems, and the more interesting an example is to someone, the more specialized it tends to be. Trouble is, such examples usually address arcane problems that are hard for nonspecialists to understand.

So let's consider how we might design something every computer user should be familiar with: an hierarchical file system. We won't concern ourselves with low-level implementation issues such as I/O buffering and disk-sector management. Instead, what we'll be designing is the programming model that application writers use—the file system's application programming interface, or API. In most operating systems, this API consists of several dozen procedure calls and some data structures, with little or no provision for extension. Our design will be fully object-oriented and extensible.

I'll focus first on two particularly important aspects of the design and the patterns that address them. Then I'll build on the example to show you how other patterns address design issues. The point here is not to prescribe a rigid process for pattern application or to demonstrate the best way to design a file system; it's to encourage you to apply patterns yourself. The more you use patterns and see them used, the more comfortable you'll be with them. Eventually, you will acquire the perfect technique for applying patterns: your own.

Fundamentals

From the user's perspective, a file system should handle file structures of arbitrary size and complexity. It shouldn't put arbitrary limits on how wide or deep the file structure can get. From the programmer's perspective, the representation for the file structure should be easy to deal with and extend.

Suppose you are implementing a command that lists the files in a directory. The code you write to get the name of a *directory* shouldn't have to be different from the code you write to get the name of a *file*—the same code should work for both. In other words, you should be able to treat directories and files the same when requesting their names. The resulting code will be easier to write and maintain. You also want to accommodate new kinds of files (symbolic links, for example) without reimplementing half the system.

So two things are clear at the outset: Files and directories are key elements in the problem domain, and we need a way to introduce specialized versions of these elements after we've finalized the design. An obvious design approach is to represent the elements as objects:

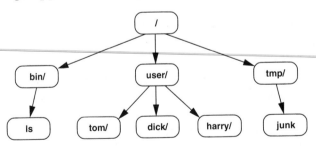

How do you implement such a structure? The fact that we have two kinds of objects suggests two classes—one for files and one for directories. We also want to treat files and directories uniformly, which means they must have a common interface. In turn, that means the classes must be derived from a common (abstract) base class, which we'll call *Node*. Last but not least, we know that directories aggregate files.

All these constraints essentially define the class hierarchy for us:

```
class Node {
public:
    // declare common interface here
protected:
    Node();
    Node(const Node&);
};
class File : public Node {
public:
    File();

    // redeclare common interface here
};
class Directory : public Node {
public:
    Directory();

    // redeclare common interface here
private:
    list<Node*> _nodes;
};
```

The next question to ponder concerns the makeup of the common interface. What are the operations that apply equally to files and directories?

Well, there are all sorts of attributes of common interest, such as name, size, protection, and so forth. Each attribute can have operations for accessing and modifying its value(s). Operations that have clear meaning for both files and directories are easy to treat uniformly. Tricky issues arise when the operations don't seem to apply so clearly to both.

For example, one of the things users do a lot is ask for a list of files in a directory. That means `Directory` needs an interface for enumerating its children. Here's a simple one that returns the *n*th child:

```
virtual Node* getChild(int n);
```

`getChild` must return a `Node*`, because the directory may contain either File objects or Directory objects. The type of that return value has an important ramification: It forces us to define getChild not just in the Directory class but in the Node class as well. Why? Because we want to be able to list the children of a *sub*directory. In fact, the user will often want to descend the file system structure. We won't be able to do that in a statically type-safe way unless we can call getChild on what getChild returns, without casting. So, like the attribute operations, getChild is something we want to apply uniformly.

getChild is also key to letting us define Directory operations recursively. Suppose Node declares a size operation that returns the total number of bytes consumed by the directory (sub)tree. Directory could define its version of this operation as a sum of the values its children return when their size operation gets called:

```
long Directory::size () {
    long total = 0;
    Node* child;

    for (int i = 0; child = getChild(i); ++i) {
        total += child->size();
    }

    return total;
}
```

Directories and files illustrate the key aspects of the COMPOSITE pattern: It yields tree structures of arbitrary complexity, and it prescribes how to treat the objects in those structures uniformly. COMPOSITE's Intent echoes these aspects:

> Compose objects into tree structures to represent part–whole hierarchies, and give clients a uniform way of dealing with these objects whether they are internal nodes or leaves.

The Applicability section states that you should use COMPOSITE when

- you want to represent part–whole hierarchies of objects.
- you want clients to be able to ignore the difference between compositions of objects and individual objects. Clients will treat all objects in the composite structure uniformly.

The pattern's Structure section presents a modified OMT diagram of the canonical COMPOSITE class structure. By *canonical* I mean simply that it represents the most common arrangement of classes that we (Gang of Four) have observed. It can't represent the *definitive* set of

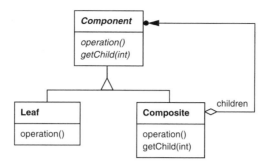

FIGURE 2.1   *COMPOSITE structure*

classes and relationships, because the interfaces may vary when we
consider certain design or implementation-driven trade-offs. (The pattern spells those out too.)

Figure 2.1 shows the classes that participate in COMPOSITE and their
static relationships. Component is the abstract base class to which our
Node class corresponds. Subclass participants are Leaf (to which File
corresponds) and Composite (Directory). The arrowhead line going
from Composite to Component reveals that Composite contains
instances of type Component. The ball at the tip of the arrowhead indicates more than one instance; if the ball were omitted, it would mean
exactly one instance. The diamond at the base of the arrowhead line
means that the Composite aggregates its child instances, which implies
that deleting a composite would delete its children as well. It also
implies that components aren't shared, thus ensuring tree structures.
The Participants and Collaborations sections of the pattern explain the
static and dynamic relationships, respectively, among these participants.

COMPOSITE's Consequences section sums up the benefits and liabilities of the pattern. On the plus side, COMPOSITE supports tree structures
of arbitrary complexity. A corollary of this property is that a node's
complexity is hidden from clients: They can't tell whether they're
dealing with a leaf or a composite component—and they don't have to,
which makes client code more independent of the code in the components. The client is also simpler, because it can treat leaves and compos-
ites uniformly. No longer do clients have to decide which of multiple

code paths to take based on the type of component. Best of all, you can add new types of components without touching existing code.

COMPOSITE's down-side, however, is that it can lead to a system in which the class of every object looks like the class of every other. Significant differences show up only at run-time, which can make the code hard to understand even if you are privy to class implementations. Moreover, the number of objects can become prohibitive if the pattern is applied at a low level or at too fine a granularity.

As you might have guessed, implementation issues abound for the COMPOSITE pattern. It discusses

- when and where to cache information to improve performance,
- how much storage the Component class should allocate,
- what data structure(s) to use for storing children,
- whether operations for adding and removing children should be declared in the Component class,
- and lots more.

We'll wrestle with some of these issues along with many others as we develop our file system.

Orphans, Adoption, and Surrogates

Now let's go a little deeper into COMPOSITE's implications in this application. We'll look at an important trade-off in the design of the Node class interface, and then we'll take a shot at adding some new functionality to our fledgling design.

We've used COMPOSITE to generate the backbone of this application. It showed us how to express the fundamental characteristics of hierarchical file systems in object-oriented terms. The pattern relates its key participants—the Component, Composite, and Leaf classes—through inheritance and composition in a way that supports file system structures of arbitrary size and complexity. It also lets clients treat files and directories (and whatever else might be in there) uniformly.

As you've seen, the key to uniformity lies in a common interface among objects in the file system. So far we have three classes of object in the design: Node, File, and Directory. I've explained how operations that have clear meaning for both files and directories need to be declared in the Node base class. Operations for getting and setting the node's name and protection fall into this category. I also explained why we need to include an operation for accessing child nodes (`get-Child`) in the common interface, even though at first glance it doesn't seem appropriate for File objects. Now we'll consider other operations that are even less obviously common.

At the risk of sounding like a precocious five-year-old, where do children come from anyway? (I guess it's a fair question in any context.) Before we can expect a Directory object to enumerate its children, it must acquire them somehow. But from where?

Clearly not from itself. The directory can't assume responsibility for creating every child it might ever contain—the user of the file system controls such things. It's reasonable to expect clients of the file system to create files and directories and then put them where they want them. That means Directory objects, in particular, will *adopt* child nodes rather than create them. Hence Directory needs an interface for adopting children. Something like

```
virtual void adopt(Node* child);
```

will do.

When a client calls `adopt` on a directory, the client is explicitly handing over responsibility for the given child to the directory. Responsibility implies ownership: When the directory gets deleted, the child does also. This is the essence of the aggregation relationship (denoted by the diamond in Figure 2.1) between the Directory and Node classes.

Now, if a client can tell a directory to assume responsibility for a child, a call to *relinquish* such responsibility is in order. Hence:

```
virtual void orphan(Node* child);
```

In this case "orphan" doesn't imply that the parent directory dies . . . er, gets deleted. It just means the directory is no longer the child's parent. The child lives on too, perhaps soon to be adopted by another node, perhaps to be . . . deleted.

So what does this have to do with uniformity? Why can't we define these operations on Directory and nowhere else?

Okay, say we do that. Now consider how a client implements operations that change the file system structure. An example of such a client is a user-level command that creates a new directory. The user interface for this command is immaterial; let's assume it's just a command-line interface like the UNIX mkdir command. mkdir takes a name for the directory-to-be as an argument, like so:

```
mkdir newsubdir
```

Actually, the user can prepend any valid path to the name:

```
mkdir subdirA/subdirB/newsubdir
```

This should work so long as subdirA and subdirB exist and are directories, as opposed to files. More generally, subdirA and subdirB should be instances of Node subclasses that can have children. If this isn't true, then the user should get an error message.

How do we implement mkdir? First, let's assume mkdir can find out what the current directory is; that is, it can obtain a reference to the Directory object that corresponds to the user's choice of current directory.[1] Adding a new directory to the current one is simply a matter of creating a new Directory instance and then calling adopt on the current directory, passing the new directory as a parameter:

```
Directory* current;
// ...
current->adopt(new Directory("newsubdir"));
```

Easy. But what about the general case, where mkdir is supplied a nontrivial path?

This is where things get trickier. mkdir must

1. Find the subdirA object (reporting an error if it doesn't exist).

2. Find the subdirB object (reporting an error if it doesn't exist).

3. Have the subdirB object adopt the newsubdir object.

---

1. The client could get the current directory object from a well-known place, such as a static operation on the Node class. Accessing well-known resources is a job for the SINGLETON design pattern. We'll see it in action later.

Items 1 and 2 involve iterating through the children of the current directory and those of subdirA (if it exists) in search of a node representing subdirB.

At the heart of mkdir's implementation might be a recursive function that takes a path as an argument:

```
void Client::mkdir (
    Directory* current, const string& path
) {
    string subpath = subpath(path);

    if (subpath.empty()) {
        current->adopt(new Directory(path));

    } else {
        string name = head(path);
        Node* child = find(name, current);

        if (child) {
            mkdir(child, subpath);
        } else {
            cerr << name << " nonexistent." << endl;
        }
    }
}
```

where head and subpath are string manipulation routines. head returns the first name in the path; subpath returns everything else. The find operation searches a directory for a child of a given name:

```
Node* Client::find (
    const string& name, Directory* current
) {
    Node* child = 0;

    for (int i = 0; child = current->getChild(i); ++i) {
        if (name == child->getName()) {
            return child;
        }
    }
    return 0;
}
```

Note that find must return a Node*, because that's what getChild returns. There's nothing unreasonable about that, since a child can be either a directory or a file. But if you've been paying attention, you will have noticed that this little detail effectively sinks `Client::mkdir`—it won't compile.

Look again at the recursive call to `mkdir`. It's passed a `Node*`, not the `Directory*` it needs. The problem is that when we descend the hierarchy, we can't tell whether a child is a file or a directory. Generally this is a Good Thing, as long as clients don't care about the difference. But in this case it seems we do indeed care, because only `Directory` defines an interface for adopting and orphaning children.

But do we *really* care? Or more to the point, does the client (the `mkdir` command) need to care? Not really. Its charter is to either create a new directory or report failure to the user. So suppose—just suppose—we treat `adopt` and `orphan` uniformly across Node classes.

I know, I know. You're thinking, "Egad! Those operations don't mean anything for leaf components like File." But how practical is that assumption? What if down the road someone else defines a new kind of leaf component like a trash can (or, more correctly, a recycle bin) that annihilates whatever it adopts? What if adopting into a leaf means "generate an error message"? It's hard to prove that `adopt` can never make sense for leaves. Same for `orphan`.

On the other hand, it might make sense to argue that there's no need for separate File and Directory classes in the first place—*everything* should be a Directory. But implementation issues argue differently. Directory objects tend to have baggage that most files don't need: a data structure for storing children, cached child information for improved performance, and so forth. Experience shows that, in many applications, leaves tend to be more plentiful than internal nodes. That's one reason why COMPOSITE prescribes separate Leaf and Composite classes.

Let's see what happens when we define `adopt` and `orphan` on *all* Nodes instead of just the Directory class. We'll make these operations generate error messages by default:

```
virtual void Node::adopt (Node*) {
    cerr << getName() << " is not a directory." << endl;
}
virtual void Node::orphan (Node* child) {
    cerr << child->getName() << " not found." << endl;
}
```

These aren't necessarily the best error messages, but you get the idea. Alternatively, these operations could throw exceptions, or they could do nothing—there are lots of possibilities. In any event, `Client::mkdir` now works beautifully.[2] Notice also that this approach required no change to the File class. We do of course have to change `Client::mkdir` to take a `Node*` instead of a `Directory*`:

```
void Client::mkdir (Node* current, const string& path) {
    // ...
}
```

Here's the point: Although `adopt` and `orphan` might not seem to be operations we should treat uniformly, there's real benefit in doing so, at least in this application. The most likely alternative would have been to introduce some sort of downcast that lets the client identify the type of node:

```
void Client::mkdir (
    Directory* current, const string& path
) {
    string subpath = subpath(path);

    if (subpath.empty()) {
        current->adopt(new Directory(path));

    } else {
        string name = head(path);
        Node* node = find(name, current);

        if (node) {
            Directory* child =
                dynamic_cast<Directory*>(node);

            if (child) {
                mkdir(child, subpath);
```

---

2. Well, *almost* beautifully. I confess I've ignored memory management issues in this example. Specifically, we have a potential memory leak when `adopt` gets called on a leaf, because the client passes ownership to a node that won't accept ownership. This is a general problem with `adopt`, because it could fail even on Directory objects (when the client has insufficient permission, for example). The problem goes away when Nodes are reference counted, and `adopt` decrements (or doesn't increment) the reference count on failure.

```
        } else {
            cerr << getName()
                    << " is not a directory."
                    << endl;
        }
    } else {
        cerr << name << " nonexistent." << endl;
    }
  }
}
```

See how the `dynamic_cast` introduced an extra control path? It's needed to handle the case where the user specified an invalid directory name somewhere in `path`. This illustrates how nonuniformity can make clients more complicated.

That's not to say there's never a good reason for nonuniformity. In some applications it may be imperative for the compiler to detect any attempt to call child operations on a leaf. `adopt`, `orphan`, and operations like them cannot be declared in the base class in such cases. But in situations where there are no dire consequences to guard against, uniformity usually pays dividends in simplicity and extensibility, as we will soon see.

"But Where Do Surrogates Fit into This?"

Glad you asked, because it's time we looked at adding a new feature—namely, symbolic links (a.k.a. "aliases" in Mac Finder parlance or "shortcuts" in Windows 95). A *symbolic link* is basically a reference to another node in the file system. It's a "surrogate" for that node; it's not the node itself. If you delete the symbolic link, it goes away without affecting the node to which it refers.

A symbolic link has its own access rights, which may differ from the node's. For the most part, however, the symbolic link behaves just like the node itself. If the link refers to a file, then a client can treat the link as if it were that file; the client can edit the file and perhaps even save it through the link, for example. If the link refers to a directory, a client can add and remove nodes from the directory by performing operations on the link just as though it were the directory itself.

Symbolic links are convenient. They let you access far-flung files and directories without moving or copying them, which is great for nodes that must live in one place but get used in another. We'd be remiss if our design didn't support symbolic links.

So the first question that someone who paid good money for *Design Patterns* should ask is: Is there a pattern that helps me design and implement symbolic links? In fact, there's a bigger question: How do I find the right design pattern for the task at hand?

Section 1.7 in *Design Patterns* suggests the following six approaches:

1. Consider how design patterns solve design problems. (In other words, study Section 1.6. But you and I know how likely we are to do that in the heat of development.)

2. Scan the Intent sections for something that sounds right. (A mite brute-force.)

3. Study how patterns interrelate. (Still too involved for us here, but we're getting warmer.)

4. Look at patterns whose purpose (creational, structural, behavioral) corresponds to what you're trying to do. (Hmm, adding symbolic links to a file system suggests a structural purpose.)

5. Examine a relevant cause of redesign (listed in *Design Patterns* starting on page 24), and apply the patterns that help you avoid it. (Seems a little early for *re*design given we don't have a *design* yet.)

6. Consider what should be variable in your design. For each design pattern, Table 1.2 on page 30 of *Design Patterns* lists one or more design aspects that the pattern lets you vary.

Let's pursue that last item. If we look at the structural patterns in Table 1.2, we see that

- ADAPTER lets you vary the interface to an object.
- BRIDGE lets you vary the implementation of an object.
- COMPOSITE lets you vary an object's structure and composition.
- DECORATOR lets you vary responsibilities without subclassing.
- FACADE lets you vary the interface to a subsystem.
- FLYWEIGHT lets you vary storage costs of objects.
- PROXY lets you vary how an object is accessed and/or its location.

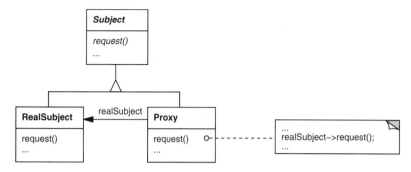

FIGURE 2.2 *PROXY structure*

Maybe I'm biased, but it sure sounds like PROXY is our pattern. Turning there, we find the following Intent:

> Provide a surrogate or placeholder for another object to control access to it.

The Motivation section applies the pattern to the problem of delayed loading of images (not unlike what you'd want in a Web browser, for example).

But it's the Applicability section that clinches it for us. It states that PROXY is applicable whenever you need a more versatile or sophisticated reference to an object than a simple pointer. It goes on to list some common situations in which it applies, including a "protection proxy" that controls access to another object—just what we need.

All right, now how do we apply the PROXY pattern to our file system design? Looking at the pattern's Structure diagram (Figure 2.2), you'll see three key classes: an abstract Subject class, a concrete RealSubject subclass, and another concrete Proxy subclass. Hence we can conclude that Subject, RealSubject, and Proxy have compatible interfaces. The Proxy subclass also contains a reference to RealSubject. The pattern's Participants section explains that the Proxy class provides an identical interface to Subject's, which lets a Proxy object substitute for any subject. Further, RealSubject is the type of object that the proxy represents.

Mapping these relationships back to our file system classes, it's clear that the common interface we want to adhere to is Node's. (That's what the COMPOSITE pattern taught us, after all.) This suggests that the Node class plays the part of Subject in the pattern.

Next we need to define a Node subclass corresponding to the Proxy class in the pattern. I'll call it *Link*:

```
class Link : public Node {
public:
    Link(Node*);

    // redeclare common Node interface here

private:
    Node* _subject;
};
```

The `_subject` member provides the reference to the real subject. But it seems we're deviating a bit from the pattern's Structure diagram, which would have the reference be of type RealSubject. In our case that would correspond to a reference of type File or Directory, yet we want symbolic links to work for either kind of Node. What to do?

If you look at the pattern's description of the Proxy participant, you'll find these words:

> [Proxy] maintains a reference that lets the proxy access the real subject. Proxy may refer to a Subject if the RealSubject and Subject interfaces are the same.

Given all we've talked about so far, it is indeed the case that File and Directory share the Node interface. Therefore `_subject` is a pointer to a Node. Without a common interface, it's much harder to define a symbolic link that works for both files and directories. In fact, you'd probably end up defining two kinds of symbolic links that work identically, save that one is for files and the other is for directories.

The last major issue to address concerns how Link implements the Node interface. To first approximation it merely delegates each operation to the corresponding operation on `_subject`. It might delegate `getChild` like this:

```
Node* Link::getChild (int n) {
    return _subject->getChild(n);
}
```

In some cases the Link may exhibit behavior independent of its subject. For example, Link might define protection operations of its own, in which case it could implement those operations just like File does.

❖ ❖ ❖

Laurion Burchall had some astute observations about the PROXY pattern in this application [Burchall95]:

> If a file is deleted, the proxies pointing to it will have dangling pointers. The OBSERVER pattern could be used to notify all proxies when a file is deleted, but this does not allow us to move a new file into the old file's location and have symbolic links still work.
>
> In UNIX and the Mac, symbolic links hold the actual name of the file they reference, not something more concrete. The proxy could hold the name of the file and a reference to the root of the file system. This could make accessing a file through the proxy expensive, though, as a name lookup would have to be performed each time.

All quite true—except the part about OBSERVER. There's no reason a proxy couldn't be notified and reattached when the file it points to gets replaced. Replacement is analogous to deletion in that regard.

But Laurion's point is well-taken: Keeping just a pointer to the subject, while efficient, is indeed likely to be unsatisfactory without added mechanism. Replacing a subject without invalidating links to it calls for a level of indirection we don't currently have. Storing the file's name instead of a pointer will work, but it may necessitate some kind of associative store to map the name back to the object efficiently. Even then, there's overhead compared to storing a pointer; but it shouldn't be a problem unless there are links to too many files, or you have too many levels of links. Of course, the associative store also will have to be updated whenever files are deleted or replaced.

I like to make the common case fast at the uncommon case's expense. If accessing a file through a link is more common than replacing or deleting the file, as I suspect it is, then an OBSERVER-based approach would be preferable to a name lookup.

As a design like this evolves, one of the things to watch out for is the tendency to treat the base class as a dumping ground: Its interface grows as operations accumulate over time. An operation or two gets added with each new file system feature. Today it's support for extended attributes; next week it's calculating a new kind of size statistic; next month it's an operation that returns an icon for a graphical

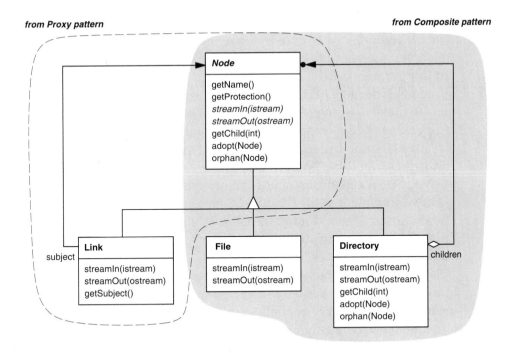

from Proxy pattern   *from Composite pattern*

FIGURE 2.3   *Class structure embodying* COMPOSITE *and* PROXY

user interface. Before long, Node is a behemoth of a class—tough to understand, maintain, and subclass.

I'll address this problem next. We'll look at a way to add new operations to our design without modifying existing classes at all.

Visiting Rights

So far we've applied two design patterns: We used COMPOSITE to define the structure of the file system, and PROXY showed us how to support symbolic links. Incorporating the changes we've discussed so far, along with a few other refinements, gives us the class hierarchy shown in Figure 2.3.

getName and getProtection return the corresponding attributes of the node. The Node base class defines default implementations for these operations. streamIn and streamOut are operations for streaming a node's contents into and out of the file system. (We'll assume that files are modeled as simple bytestreams, as in UNIX.) streamIn and streamOut are *abstract* operations, meaning that the base class declares but doesn't necessarily implement them. As such their names appear in slanted type. getChild, adopt, and orphan have default implementations to make defining leaf components a bit easier.

Speaking of leaf components, recall that the Node, File, and Directory classes came from COMPOSITE. PROXY contributed the Link class, and it prescribed the Node class, which we already had. As a result, the Node class constitutes a junction of sorts between the two patterns: It's the Component in the COMPOSITE pattern, and it's the Subject in the PROXY pattern. Such dual citizenship is the mark of what Alexander calls a "dense" composition of patterns, where two or more occupy the same "space" of classes in the system.

Density has its pluses and minuses. Having multiple patterns dwell in relatively few classes lends a certain profundity to a design; much meaning is captured in a small space, not unlike good poetry. On the other hand, such density can be reminiscent of less inspired efforts.

Richard Gabriel puts it this way [Gabriel95]:

> [Alexandrian density] in software corresponds at least partly to highly bummed code—code where each part is doing more than one thing. Code like the code you produce when your first cut at it is two to three times too big for the RAM it needs to occupy, code like we used to have to write in the '60s and '70s in assembler.

Good point—"profound" code isn't necessarily good code. Actually, Richard's concern is symptomatic of a larger problem: The pattern can get lost after it's been implemented. There's a lot to talk about here, but it'll have to wait—our file system beckons!

In an operating system, the vast majority of user-level commands deal with the file system in some way. And no wonder; the file system is *the* repository of information in the computer. Such a central component is bound to engender new functionality as the operating system evolves.

The classes we've defined so far provide a modicum of functionality. In particular, the Node class interface encompasses just a few fundamental operations that all Node subclasses support. These operations are fundamental in that they give you access to information and behavior that only a node can furnish.

Naturally, there are other operations you might want to perform on these classes. Consider an operation for counting the number of words in a file. Once we recognize that we need such a thing, we might be tempted to add a "getWordCount" operation to the Node base class. And that would be a Bad Thing, because we would end up modifying the File class at least and probably every other class as well. We'd really *really* like to avoid modifying (read "adding bugs to") existing code. There's no need to panic, however, for we have streaming operations in the base class. A client of the file system can use them to examine the text in a file. We're saved from changing existing code because clients can implement word count in terms of existing operations.

In fact, I'll assert that the primary challenge when designing the Node interface is to come up with a minimal set of operations that lets clients build open-ended functionality. The alternative—performing surgery on Node and its subclasses for each new capability—is both invasive and error-prone. It also makes the Node interface evolve into a hodgepodge of operations, eventually obscuring the essential properties of Node objects. The classes get hard to understand, hard to extend, and hard to use. So focusing on a sufficient set of primitives is key to defining a simple, coherent Node interface.

But what about operations that should work differently on different kinds of nodes—how can you make them external to Node classes? Take the UNIX `cat` command, for instance. It simply prints the contents of a file to standard output. But when it's applied to a directory, it reports that the node cannot be printed, probably because a directory's textual representation doesn't look too pretty.

Because `cat`'s behavior depends on the type of node, it seems necessary to define a base-class operation that Files and Directories implement differently. So we end up changing existing classes after all.

Is there an alternative? Suppose we insist on taking this functionality out of the Node classes and putting it into a client. Then it seems there's no choice but to introduce some kind of downcast to let the client figure out what kind of node it's dealing with:

```
void Client::cat (Node* node) {
    Link* l;

    if (dynamic_cast<File*>(node)) {
        node->streamOut(cout); // stream out contents
    } else if (dynamic_cast<Directory*>(node)) {
        cerr << "Can't cat a directory." << endl;
    } else if (l = dynamic_cast<Link*>(node)) {
        cat(l->getSubject());  // cat the link's subject
    }
}
```

Once again, the downcast seems unavoidable. And once again, it makes the client more complicated. True, we're deliberately putting functionality into the client instead of the Node classes. But in addition to the functionality itself, we're adding type tests and conditional branches—which amounts to a second level of method dispatch.

If putting the functionality into the Nodes themselves is distasteful, then resorting to a downcast seems downright yucky. But before we blithely hack a cat() operation into Node and its subclasses to avoid the downcast, let's look at VISITOR, a design pattern that offers a third alternative. Its Intent goes like this:

> Represent an operation to be performed on the elements of an object structure. VISITOR lets you define a new operation without changing the classes of the elements on which it operates.

The pattern's Motivation section talks about a compiler that represents programs in terms of abstract syntax trees. The problem there is to support an open-ended set of analyses, such as type checking, pretty printing, and code generation, without changing the classes that implement the abstract syntax trees. The compiler problem is analogous to our own, except that we're operating on file system structures instead of abstract syntax trees; and we want to do rather different things to our structures. (Then again, maybe pretty-printing a directory structure isn't so farfetched.) In any case, the operations themselves don't really matter. What does matter is separating them from Node classes without resorting to downcasts and extra control paths.

VISITOR achieves this by adding just one operation to what it calls the "Element" participant, which in our context is the Node class:

```
virtual void accept(Visitor&) = 0;
```

accept lets a "Visitor" object visit a given node. The Visitor object encapsulates the operation to perform on the node. All concrete Element subclasses implement accept in the same simple way:

```
void File::accept (Visitor& v)      { v.visit(this); }
void Directory::accept (Visitor& v) { v.visit(this); }
void Link::accept (Visitor& v)      { v.visit(this); }
```

All these implementations look the same, but of course they're really different—the type of this is different in each case. The implementations suggest the Visitor interface looks something like this:

```
class Visitor {
public:
    Visitor();

    void visit(File*);
    void visit(Directory*);
    void visit(Link*);
};
```

The interesting property here is that when a node's accept operation calls visit on the Visitor object, the node effectively identifies its type to the Visitor. In turn, the Visitor operation that's called can do whatever is appropriate for that type of node:

```
void Visitor::visit (File* f) {
    f->streamOut(cout);
}

void Visitor::visit (Directory* d) {
    cerr << "Can't cat a directory." << endl;
}

void Visitor::visit (Link* l) {
    l->getSubject()->accept(*this);
}
```

The last operation merits some explanation. It calls `getSubject()`, which returns the node that the link points to—that is, its subject.[3] We can't simply tell the subject to stream itself out, because it might be a directory. Instead, we tell it to accept the visitor just like we did for the link itself. That lets the visitor act according to the type of subject. The visitor follows any number of links in this way until it reaches a file or a directory, where it can finally do something useful.

So now we can `cat` any node simply by creating a visitor and telling the node to accept it:

```
Visitor cat;
node->accept(cat);
```

The node's call back on the visitor resolves to the `visit` operation that corresponds to the node's actual type (File, Directory, or Link), thereby eliciting the appropriate response. The bottom line is that this Visitor can package up functionality like the `cat` command in a single class without resorting to type tests.

Encapsulating the `cat` operation in `Visitor` is neat, but it still looks as though we have to change existing code if we want to do something other than `cat` the file. Suppose we want to implement another command that lists the names of children in a directory, like the UNIX `ls` command. Further, the name that's output should be suffixed by a slash (/) if the node is a directory or by an at sign (@) if it's a symbolic link.

We need to give another Visitor-like class "visiting rights" to Nodes, but we don't want to add another `accept` operation to the Node base class. And we don't have to. Any Node object can accept any type of Visitor object. It's just that right now we have only one kind of Visitor. In the VISITOR pattern, however, `Visitor` is actually an abstract class:

```
class Visitor {
public:
    virtual ~Visitor() { }

    virtual void visit(File*) = 0;
    virtual void visit(Directory*) = 0;
    virtual void visit(Link*) = 0;
```

---

3. `getSubject()` is specific to the `Link` class; only the `Link` class declares and implements it. So we can't access that operation when we treat links as nodes. But this isn't a problem when we use a Visitor, which in effect recovers type information when it visits a node.

```
protected:
    Visitor();
    Visitor(const Visitor&);
};
```

You subclass Visitor for each new capability, implementing the visit operations appropriately for every kind of node that can be visited. A CatVisitor subclass, for example, implements the operations as before. We can also define a SuffixPrinterVisitor that prints the appropriate suffix for a node:

```
class SuffixPrinterVisitor : public Visitor {
public:
    SuffixPrinterVisitor() { }
    virtual ~SuffixPrinterVisitor() { }

    virtual void visit(File*)      { }
    virtual void visit(Directory*) { cout << "/"; }
    virtual void visit(Link*)      { cout << "@"; }
};
```

We can use SuffixPrinterVisitor in a client that implements the ls command:

```
void Client::ls (Node* n) {
    SuffixPrinterVisitor suffixPrinter;
    Node* child;

    for (int i = 0; child = n->getChild(i); ++i) {
        cout << child->getName();
        child->accept(suffixPrinter);
        cout << endl;
    }
}
```

Once we establish visiting rights by adding accept(Visitor&) to Node classes, we needn't modify those classes ever again, no matter how many Visitor subclasses we define.

We've used function overloading to give the Visitor operations the same name. An alternative is to encode the type of node in the visit operation's name:

```
class Visitor {
public:
    virtual ~Visitor() { }
```

```
        virtual void visitFile(File*) = 0;
        virtual void visitDirectory(Directory*) = 0;
        virtual void visitLink(Link*) = 0;
    protected:
        Visitor();
        Visitor(const Visitor&);
    };
```

Calls to these operations become a little clearer, if more verbose:

```
void File::accept (Visitor& v) { v.visitFile(this); }
```

```
void Directory::accept (Visitor& v) {
    v.visitDirectory(this);
}
```

```
void Link::accept (Visitor& v) { v.visitLink(this); }
```

A more substantial advantage comes when there's reasonable default behavior, and subclasses tend to override just a few of the operations. When we overload, subclasses must override *all* of the functions; otherwise your friendly C++ compiler will probably complain that your selective overrides hide one or more of the base class operations. We get around this problem when we give Visitor operations different names. Subclasses can then redefine a subset of the operations with impunity.

The base class operations may implement default behavior for each type of node. When the default behavior is common to two or more types, we can put the common functionality into a "catch-all" visitNode(Node*) operation for other operations to call by default:

```
void Visitor::visitNode (Node* n) {
    // common default behavior
}
void Visitor::visitFile (File* f) {
    Visitor::visitNode(f);
}
void Visitor::visitDirectory (Directory* d) {
    Visitor::visitNode(d);
}
void Visitor::visitLink (Link* l) {
    Visitor::visitNode(l);
}
```

VISITOR *Caveats*

There are a couple of things to consider before you apply the VISITOR pattern.

First, ask yourself, Is the class hierarchy I'm visiting stable? In our case, are we constantly defining new Node subclasses, or is that a rarity? Adding a new kind of Node may force us to change all the classes in the Visitor hierarchy just to add a corresponding `visit` operation.

If none of your visitors care about the new subclass, and you've defined the equivalent of a `visitNode` operation that provides reasonable default behavior, then there's no problem. But if just one kind of visitor does care, then at the least you'll have to change both it and the Visitor base class. Then again, maybe multiple changes are inevitable in such circumstances. If you didn't use VISITOR but instead lumped the functionality into the Node hierarchy, you'd probably end up making several changes to that too.

The second thing to realize is that VISITOR creates a circular dependency between Visitor and Node class hierarchies. Consequently, a change to either base class interface is likely to prompt a recompile of both hierarchies. Again, this probably isn't much worse than changing a lumped base class. But, in general, you want to avoid such dependencies.

Here's a relevant insight from Kevlin Henney [Henney96]:

C++'s overloading does not require having to overload all versions of `visit` or that you abandon overloading the `visit` member.

As well as supporting namespace concepts, the `using` declaration allows you to inject names from a base class into the current class for overloading:

```
class NewVisitor : public Visitor {
public:
    using Visitor::visit; // pull in all visit
                          // functions for overloading

    virtual void visit(Node*); // override Node* variant
};
```

This maintains the regularity that overloading offers. It is noninvasive as users are not forced to remember what names or convention to use for the [visit] function; it allows a newer release of Visitor to incorporate changes without affecting client code.

We've looked at patterns (COMPOSITE and PROXY) for defining the file system structure and a pattern (VISITOR) for introducing new capabilities noninvasively, that is, by *adding* code rather than *changing* code. Here lies another bromide of good object-oriented design: You maximize flexibility and maintainability when your system can be modified without touching existing code. If you can still say that after others have leveraged your software, then congratulations—you've delivered on much of the promise of object technology!

But I digress. Another major design issue in our file system has to do with security. There are at least two relevant subissues:

1. Protecting the system from inadvertent and malicious corruption.

2. Maintaining system integrity in the face of hardware and software errors.

I'll focus on the first of these subissues here, leaving the second to you as an exercise. (If you take that as a challenge, I'll be more than happy to grade your solution.)

Single-User Protection

Anyone who's used a computer extensively has a horror story to tell about how he or she lost vital data through an unfortunate syntax error, a wayward mouse click, or just one of those late-night brain-faults. Deleting the wrong file at the right time is a common catastrophe. Another is inadvertent editing—changing a file that shouldn't be changed casually. While a truly advanced file system would have an undo feature for recovering from such mishaps, prevention is usually preferable to cure. Sadly, most file systems give you a different choice: prevention or regret.

For now I'll concentrate on protecting file system objects (i.e., nodes) from deletion and modification. I'll consider protection as it relates to the programming interface rather than the user interface. The distinction needn't worry us anyway, since our programming abstractions correspond closely to user-level abstractions. Also I assume we're dealing with a single-user file system like you'd find on a classic, non-networked personal computer (as opposed to a multiuser one, such as UNIX). That will keep things simple at the outset. I'll consider the implications of multiuser protection later.

All elements of the file system (including files, directories, and symbolic links) adhere to the Node interface, which currently includes the following operations:[4]

```
const string& getName();
const Protection& getProtection();

void setName(const string&);
void setProtection(const Protection&);

void streamIn(istream&);
void streamOut(ostream&);

Node* getChild(int);

void adopt(Node*);
void orphan(Node*);
```

I've said something substantive about each of these operations except getProtection. Ostensibly it retrieves a node's protection information, but what that means isn't clear yet. What kind of protection are we talking about?

If we're aiming to protect nodes from accidental change or deletion, then all we need is write protection—that is, the node can be either writable or unwritable. If we stipulate further that the node should be protected from prying eyes, then we should be able to make it unreadable as well. Of course, that will only protect it from eyes that are both prying and *ignorant*—ignorant of how one changes a node's protection. Read protection might be useful for keeping stuff away from your spouse and maybe even your kids, but it isn't exactly indispensable. It will become more important in a multiuser environment.

---

4. Note that I've added corresponding set... operations for getName and getProtection. They do what you'd expect.

To recap, we know that nodes can be readable or unreadable, writable or unwritable. Most file systems have additional protection modes governing things like executability, automatic archiving, and whatever else. We can treat those kinds of protection in more or less the same way as readability and writability. I'll limit the discussion to these two modes to get the point across.

What effect do unreadability and unwritability have on a node's behavior? Obviously, an unreadable file shouldn't reveal its contents, which suggests that it shouldn't respond to streamOut requests. Perhaps less obviously, a client shouldn't have access to the children of an unreadable node, if it has any. So getChild should be inoperative for the unreadable node. As for unwritability, an unwritable node should let you change neither its attributes nor its structure; hence setName, streamIn, adopt, and orphan should be neutralized as well. (setProtection must be treated gingerly in this regard. I'll talk more about that when we get to multiuser protection.)

Preventing the deletion of an unwritable node poses some interesting language-level challenges. For example, a client can't explicitly delete a node like other objects. The C++ compiler can catch such an attempt for us, but not by declaring a node const, as one might be inclined. A node's protection can change at run-time, after all.

Instead, we can *protect the destructor*. Unlike a normal public destructor, a protected destructor makes it illegal for classes outside the Node class hierarchy to delete a node explicitly.[5] Protecting the destructor also has the nice property of disallowing local Node objects, that is, nodes created on the stack. It prevents an unwritable node from getting deleted automatically when it goes out of scope—an inconsistency that might indicate a bug.

But how do you (attempt to) delete a node now that its destructor is protected? One thing seems certain: We'll end up using some kind of operation that takes the node to be deleted as a parameter. The burning question is, who defines that operation? There are three possibilities:

1. The Node class (possibly redefined by subclasses)

2. A class outside the Node class hierarchy

3. A global function

---

5. Making the destructor private isn't an option because it would disallow subclassing.

We can dismiss the third option immediately, as it provides little over a static member function defined on an existing class. A deletion operation outside the Node hierarchy is rather unappealing as well, in that it forces the class defining that operation to be a friend of Node. Why? Because if the node happens to be writable, and therefore deletable, then someone must call its protected destructor. The only way to accomplish this outside the Node class hierarchy is to make the deleting class a friend of Node. That has the unfortunate side effect of exposing not just the Node's destructor but everything else it encapsulates as well.

Let's consider the first alternative: defining a `destroy` operation on the Node base class. If we make `destroy` a static operation, then it must take a Node instance as a parameter; if it isn't static, then it can be parameterless, because the `this` parameter is implied. Choosing between static, virtual, and nonvirtual member functions boils down to a choice between extensibility and aesthetics.

A virtual member function is extensible through subclassing. But some people find the syntax

```
node->destroy();
```

a bit unsettling. I'm not sure why that is, but I bet people wince at

```
delete this;
```

for the same reason. Too suicidal, perhaps. A static member function can steer clear of this stumbling block . . .

```
Node::destroy(node);
```

. . . but it doesn't lend itself to modification in subclasses. A nonvirtual member function, meanwhile, offers the worst of both worlds.

Let's see if we can have our cake and eat it too—enjoying the syntactic advantages of a static member function while allowing extension in subclasses.

What is our `destroy` operation's charter anyhow, ignoring for a moment how subclasses might want to extend it? Two things seem invariant: `destroy` must check whether the node it's passed is writable, and if it is, `destroy` deletes it. Subclasses might want to extend the deletion criteria, or they might want to change how deletion is carried out. But the invariants remain, well, invariant. We just need a little help implementing them in an extensible way.

Enter the TEMPLATE METHOD design pattern, whose Intent reads:

Define the skeleton of an algorithm in an operation, deferring some steps to subclasses. TEMPLATE METHOD lets subclasses redefine certain steps of an algorithm without changing the algorithm's structure.

According to the first bullet of the pattern's Applicability section, TEMPLATE METHOD is applicable whenever you want to implement the invariant parts of an algorithm once and leave it up to subclasses to implement the behavior that can vary. A template method generally looks like this:

```
void BaseClass::templateMethod () {
    // an invariant part goes here
    doSomething();        // a part subclasses can vary
    // another invariant part goes here
    doSomethingElse();  // another variable part
    // and so forth
}
```

BaseClass defines the doSomething and doSomethingElse operations to implement default behavior, and subclasses specialize them to do different things. The pattern calls such operations *primitive operations*, because the template method effectively composes them to create a higher-order operation.

Primitive operations should be declared virtual, since subclasses must be able to redefine them polymorphically. The pattern suggests we identify primitive operations explicitly by prepending "do-" to their names. We should also declare them protected to keep clients from calling them directly, as they might not make sense outside the template method's context.

As for the template method itself, the pattern recommends it be declared nonvirtual (or final in Java) to ensure that the invariant parts stay invariant. We've gone a step further in our case: Our candidate for a template method, the destroy operation, is not just nonvirtual—it's static. Although that doesn't mean we can't apply the pattern, it does put a twist on our implementation of it.

But before finalizing `destroy`, let's design our primitive operations. We've already established the invariant parts of the operations, that is, determining whether the node is writable and if so, deleting it. It's not a big leap from there to the following structure:

```
void Node::destroy (Node* node) {
    if (node->isWritable()) {
        delete node;

    } else {
        cerr << node->getName() << " cannot be deleted."
            << endl;
    }
}
```

`isWritable` is a primitive operation[6] that subclasses can redefine to vary the protection criteria. The base class might provide a default implementation of `isWritable`, or it may force subclasses to implement `isWritable` by declaring it pure virtual:

```
class Node {
public:
    static void destroy(Node*);
    // ...

protected:
    virtual ~Node();
    virtual bool isWritable() = 0;
    // ...
};
```

The pure virtual declaration avoids storing protection-related state in the abstract base class, but it also precludes reusing that state in subclasses.

Although `destroy` is static rather than nonvirtual, it can still work as a template method in this case. That's because it doesn't need to refer to `this`; it merely delegates to the Node instance it's passed. And since `destroy` is a member of the Node base class, it can call protected operations, such as `isWritable` and `delete`, on Node instances without breaching encapsulation.

---

6. Okay, so I'm bending the rules. But "doIsWritable" is just too much.

Right now `destroy` uses just one primitive operation, not counting the destructor. We should add another primitive to let subclasses vary the error message rather than hard-wiring it in the base class:

```
void Node::destroy (Node* node) {
    if (node->isWritable()) {
        delete node;

    } else {
        node->doWarning(undeletableWarning);
    }
}
```

`doWarning` abstracts how the node warns the user of *any* problem, not just an inability to delete. It can be arbitrarily sophisticated, doing anything from printing a string to throwing an exception. It avoids having to define a primitive operation for every conceivable situation (such as `doUndeletableWarning`, `doUnwritableWarning`, `doThisThatOrThe-OtherWarning`, ad nauseam).

We can apply TEMPLATE METHOD to other `Node` operations, which don't happen to be static. In doing so, we introduce new primitive operations:

```
void Node::streamOut (ostream& out) {
    if (isReadable()) {
        doStreamOut(out);

    } else {
        doWarning(unreadableWarning);
    }
}
```

The major difference between the `streamOut` and `destroy` template methods is that `streamOut` can call `Node` operations directly. `destroy` can't do that because it's static and can't refer to `this`. Hence `destroy` must be passed the node to be deleted, to which it delegates the primitive operations. Remember too that `streamOut` became *non*virtual when it graduated to template method status.

❖　❖　❖

The TEMPLATE METHOD pattern leads to an inversion of control known as the *Hollywood Principle*, or, "Don't call us; we'll call you." Subclasses can extend or reimplement the variable parts of the algorithm, but they cannot alter the template method's flow of control and other invariant parts. Therefore, when you define a new subclass of Node, you have to think not in terms of control flow but *responsibility*—the operations you *must* override, those you *might* override, and others you *must not* override. Structuring your operations as template methods makes these responsibilities more explicit.

The Hollywood Principle is especially interesting because it is a key to understanding frameworks. It lets a framework capture architectural and implementation artifacts that don't vary, deferring the variant parts to application-specific subclasses.

The inversion of control is part of what makes framework programming uncomfortable for some. When programming procedurally, one is very much preoccupied with control flow. It's hard to imagine how you can understand a procedural program without knowing the twists and turns it takes, even with impeccable functional decomposition. But a good framework will abstract away control flow details. You end up focusing on objects, which by comparison can seem both more and less tangible than control flow. You must think in terms of object responsibilities and collaborations. It's a higher-level, slightly more declarative view of the world, with potentially greater leverage and flexibility. TEMPLATE METHOD realizes these benefits on a smaller scale than a framework—at the operation level rather than the object level.

Multiuser Protection

We've looked at how to add simple, single-user protection to our evolving file system design. I promised I would extend the concept to a multiuser environment, wherein users share a file system. A multiuser capability is de rigueur these days, whether you live in a traditional timesharing system with a centralized file system or a more contemporary networked file system. Even personal computer operating systems that were designed as single-user environments (like OS/2 and Windows NT) now accommodate multiple users. Whatever the context, multiuser support adds a new dimension to the protection problem.

Once again, I'll take the design path of least resistance and model our multiuser protection scheme after an existing one: that of UNIX. A node in the UNIX file system is associated with a "user." By default, the node's user is the person who created it. From the node's perspective, this association partitions the set of all users into two camps: the node's user, and everyone else. The official (and sometimes awkward) UNIX term for "everyone else" is *other*.[7]

Differentiating between a node's user and others lets us ascribe an independent protection level to each. For example, a file can be readable by its user and nobody else; we say the file is "user-readable" but "other-unreadable." Things work similarly for writability and any other protection mode we might provide, such as executability, auto-archiving, and so forth.

Users must have a *login name*, which uniquely identifies a user both to the system and to other users. To the system, the "user" and "login name" are inseparable, although in reality one human being could have multiple login names. The important thing is to ensure that a person cannot associate himself with any login name other than his own (assuming he has one). That's why you have to log-in to a UNIX system, supplying not just a login name but also a password verifying your identity. The process is known as *authentication*. UNIX goes to great lengths to guard against masquerade, since an imposter can access anything a legitimate user can.

Okay, time to get concrete. How do we model a user? Being object-oriented folk, the answer's obvious: We use an object. An object has a class, so we define the User class.

Now we need to think about an interface for the User class. Just what can clients do with a User object? Actually, the more important concern at this stage is what clients *can't* do with it. In particular, a client cannot be allowed to create User objects at will.

To understand why, let's assume there's a one-to-one correspondence between User objects and login names. (They are conceptually inseparable, and there's no clear need to allow multiple User objects for the same login name.) Assume further that a User object must always have a valid login name associated with it. That's reasonable

7. UNIX people will be quick to point out that there's a third camp, "group." We'll consider that one a bit later.

because, from the system's point of view, a user without a login name doesn't make much sense. Last but not least, we can't let a client instantiate a user without supplying both a login name *and* a password. Otherwise a rogue application could access sensitive files and directories merely by instantiating User objects with the appropriate login name.

A User object's very existence represents a unit of authentication. It's clear then that User instantiation must be a carefully controlled process. An instantiation attempt should fail if an application supplies an invalid login name or password. And it should fail without yielding half-baked User objects—that is, User objects that don't work because they were created without the requisite information. This all but rules out using conventional C++ constructors to instantiate users.

We need a secure way to create User objects that doesn't surface constructors in the client interface. By *secure* I mean there should be no way for a client to instantiate a User object illicitly. How do we express such security in object-oriented terms?

Consider the three elementary object-oriented concepts: inheritance, encapsulation, and polymorphism. The one that's arguably most relevant to security is encapsulation. *Encapsulation* is, in fact, a form of security. By definition, encapsulated code and data are guaranteed to be inaccessible to clients.[8] What then do we want to encapsulate in this case? Why, nothing less than the entire authentication process, which begins with user input and culminates in the creation of a User object.

We've homed in on the problem. Now we need to find a solution and express it in objects. Maybe it's time to look at some patterns.

At this point I'll admit we don't have a lot to guide us in our choice of pattern. But we do know that object creation figures in prominently, as does encapsulation. To help narrow the search, recall that the patterns in *Design Patterns* are grouped according to three purposes: cre-

---

8. Doug Schmidt correctly points out that such a definition can be hard to enforce in C++ [Schmidt96a]. For example, one can render all private members public with a simple #define of private to public. One way to avoid such subversions is by not declaring member variables in header files at all. Instead, you declare them along with other sensitive implementation desiderata in separate, unexported header files. A highly relevant pattern here is BRIDGE; but to paraphrase Fermat, the proof is too large for this footnote.

ational, structural, and behavioral. Of the three, the creational patterns seem most relevant here: ABSTRACT FACTORY, BUILDER, FACTORY METHOD, PROTOTYPE, and SINGLETON. Since there are only five of them, we can take a quick look at each one to decide which, if any, is appropriate.

ABSTRACT FACTORY focuses on creating families of objects without specifying their concrete classes. That's fine, but our design problem involves no notion of object "families," and we're not averse to instantiating a concrete class—namely User. So ABSTRACT FACTORY's out. Next comes BUILDER, which concerns itself with creating complex objects. It lets you use the same multistep process to construct objects having different representations . . . which isn't terribly germane either. FACTORY METHOD has an intent similar to ABSTRACT FACTORY's without the emphasis on families, making it only slightly less irrelevant.

What about PROTOTYPE? It parameterizes the kind of objects to instantiate. Instead of writing code that invokes the new operator on a class name (which can't be changed at run-time), you call a copy operation on a prototypical instance (which can be replaced at run-time). To change the class of object instantiated, simply use a different prototypical instance.

But this isn't right either. We aren't interested in changing *what* gets instantiated; we want to control *how* clients instantiate User objects. Because anyone can copy the prototypical instance, we gain precious little control compared to a plain old constructor. Besides, having a prototypical User object lying around compromises our authentication model.

That leaves SINGLETON. Its intent is to ensure a class has only one instance and to provide a global point of access to that instance. The pattern calls for a parameterless static member function called *Instance*, which returns the sole instance of the class. All constructors are protected to keep clients from using them directly.

At first this seems rather inapplicable as well—a program might need more than one User object, right? But even though we don't want to restrict the number of instances to just one, we do want to disallow more than one instance *per user*. In both cases we're limiting the number of instances.

So maybe SINGLETON is applicable after all. Looking more closely at SINGLETON's consequences, we learn the following:

[SINGLETON] permits a variable number of instances. The pattern makes it easy to change your mind and allow more than one instance of the Singleton class. Moreover, you can use the same approach to control the number of instances that the application uses. Only the [Instance] operation that grants access to the Singleton instance needs to change.

Bingo! For our variant of the pattern, we can rename the Instance operation "logIn" and give it a couple of parameters:

```
static const User* User::logIn(
    const string& loginName, const string& password
);
```

logIn ensures that only one instance is created per login name. To do that, the User class might keep a private, static hash table of User objects indexed by login name. logIn looks up the loginName parameter in this hash table. If it finds a corresponding User entry, it returns that entry; otherwise logIn does the following:

1. It creates a new User object, authenticating it against the password.

2. It registers the User object in the hash table for future accesses.

3. It returns the User object.

Here's a summary of User::logIn's properties:

- It's globally accessible.

- It prevents instantiation of more than one User object per login name.

- Unlike a constructor, it can return 0 if either the login name or the password is invalid.

- An application cannot change logIn by subclassing User.

This is admittedly an unorthodox application of SINGLETON. The fact that clients can create more than one instance of User means we aren't following the pattern's Intent to the letter. Moreover, the Implementation section spends a lot of time discussing how to subclass the Singleton class—something we surely *do not* want to allow in this application.[9]

---

9. To disallow subclassing User, just declare its constructor(s) private.

We *are* controlling the number of instances, however, and SINGLETON laid down the basic approach. Patterns aren't meant to domineer, you know. A good pattern goes beyond mere description of a solution to a problem; it'll also give you the insight and understanding to tailor the solution to your own situation.

Still, SINGLETON hasn't told us everything. For example, given that we have a `logIn` operation, it's reasonable to expect a corresponding "`logOut`" operation for logging users off the system. `logOut` raises some important issues regarding memory management for Singleton objects—issues on which SINGLETON is curiously silent. I'll expand on these issues in Chapter 3.

Next question: How does a client use a user, so to speak? To find out, let's go through a couple of use cases.

First, consider the log-in process. Assume there's a log-in program that's executed when a user wants to access the system (or at least its protected parts). The log-in program would call `User::logIn` to obtain a User object. Then, somehow, the program makes that object accessible to other applications so that the user doesn't have to log in more than once.

Second, let's think about how an application accesses a file created a few days ago by someone with the login name "johnny." Say the user of the application has login name "mom," and the file is user-readable but not other-readable. Therefore "mom" should not be allowed to access the file. In a single-user system, the application would request the contents of the file by calling its `streamOut` operation, supplying a stream:

```
void streamOut(ostream&);
```

Ideally we'd like the call to look the same in the multiuser case, but we're missing a reference to the user who's accessing the file. Without that reference, there's no way to ensure that the user has access privileges. Either the reference is supplied explicitly as a parameter . . .

```
void streamOut(ostream&, const User*);
```

. . . or it is established implicitly through the log-in process. In the common case, the application will work on behalf of one and only one user throughout its lifetime. Supplying the User object constantly as a parameter would be a nuisance in that case. However, a collaborative application could conceivably and legitimately provide access to multiple users. There, specifying the user on every operation becomes a necessity.

So there's a need to add a `const User*` parameter to each operation in the Node interface—but clients shouldn't be *forced* to supply it. Default parameters give us the flexibility to do either with grace:

```
const string& getName(const User* = 0);
const Protection& getProtection(const User* = 0);

void setName(const string&, const User* = 0);
void setProtection(const Protection&, const User* = 0);

void streamIn(istream&, const User* = 0);
void streamOut(ostream&, const User* = 0);

Node* getChild(int, const User* = 0);

void adopt(Node*, const User* = 0);
void orphan(Node*, const User* = 0);
```

In the common case, where the user is implicit, we need a globally accessible operation for retrieving the sole User instance. That amounts to a Singleton, though for flexibility we should make the Singleton instance application-settable. So instead of a single, static `User::instance` operation, we'll use static `get` and `set` operations:

```
static const User* User::getUser();
static void User::setUser(const User*);
```

setUser lets the application set the implicit user to any `const User*` it has obtained, presumably through legitimate means. Now the log-in program can call setUser to set the global User instance that other applications should use:[10]

```
extern const int maxTries;
// ...
const User* user = 0;
```

---

10. This implies that User objects live in shared memory or are otherwise transmittable between programs. An important detail, to be sure, but implementing it affects neither the interfaces we've defined nor our approach.

```
for (int i = 0; i < maxTries; ++i) {
    if (user = User::logIn(loginName, password)) {
        break;
    } else {
        cerr << "Log-in invalid!" << endl;
    }
}
if (user) {
    User::setUser(user);
} else {
    // too many unsuccessful log-in attempts;
    // lock this login name out!
    // ...
}
```

So far, so straightforward. But I've been dodging a basic question: How does all this impact the implementation of streamOut and the other template methods in Node's interface? More pointedly, how do *they* use the User object?

The key differences, compared to the single-user design, lie not in the template methods per se but in the boolean-returning primitive operations. For example, streamOut becomes

```
void Node::streamOut (ostream& out, const User* u) {
    User* user = u ? u : User::getUser();

    if (isReadableBy(user)) {
        doStreamOut(out);
    } else {
        doWarning(unreadableWarning);
    }
}
```

You'll see an obvious difference in the second line. The user local variable gets initialized to the given user or, if none was supplied, the singleton User object. But the more salient difference is in the third line, where isReadableBy has replaced isReadable. isReadableBy checks whether the node is either user-readable or other-readable, based on information stored in the node.

```
bool Node::isReadableBy (const User* user) {
    bool isOwner = user->getLoginName() == getOwner();

    return
        isOwner && isUserReadable() ||
        !isOwner && isOtherReadable();
}
```

isReadableBy reveals the need for User::getLoginName—an operation that returns the login name associated with the User object—and an interface for retrieving the login name of the node's owner:

```
const string& Node::getOwner();
```

Node also needs primitive operations like isUserReadable and isOtherReadable that provide more detailed information about readability and writability with respect to users and others. The Node base class may implement these operations as accessors to flags that it keeps in instance variables, or it may defer such storage particulars to subclasses.

Details, details. That's enough of them for now. Let's pop back up to the design level, shall we?

You'll recall that we have split the world into two camps—users and others. But that can be too all-or-nothing. If for example you're working with colleagues on a project, chances are you'll want to access each other's files. It's also possible that you'll want to protect those files from prying eyes outside your group. That's one reason UNIX provides a third protection camp: group. A *group* is a named set of login names. Making a node group-readable or -writable gives you finer control over access permission—control that maps well to a collaborative working environment.

What does it take to add a notion of groups to the design? We know two things about them:

1. Groups have zero or more users.

2. A user can be a member of zero or more groups.

Item 2 implies reference but not aggregation: Deleting a group does not delete its constituent users.

Given the way I've been talking about groups, they're just begging to be represented as objects in their own right. The question is, are we talkin' new class hierarchy here or just extendin' an existing one?

I claim the only reasonable candidate for extension is the User class. The alternative, defining a Group class as a kind of Node, is neither helpful nor meaningful. So let's consider what an inheritance relationship between Group and User might buy us.

We're already familiar with the COMPOSITE pattern. It describes the recursive relationship between Leaf nodes such as File, and Composite nodes such as Directory. It gives them identical interfaces so that we can treat them uniformly and compose them hierarchically. Perhaps what we want is a COMPOSITE relationship between users and groups: User as the Leaf class, and Group as the Composite class.

Let's refer again to COMPOSITE's Applicability section. It says the pattern is applicable when

- you want to represent part–whole hierarchies of objects.
- you want to let clients ignore the difference between compositions of objects and individual objects. Clients will treat all objects in the composite structure uniformly.

Based on these criteria, we can rest assured that the pattern is *not* applicable. Here's why:

- The relationship is not recursive. The UNIX file system doesn't allow groups of groups of groups, et cetera, and so we have no requirement for such a capability. Just because the pattern prescribes a recursive relationship doesn't mean one is needed in our application.
- A user might belong to several groups. Hence the relationship is not strictly hierarchical.
- Treating users and groups uniformly is of dubious value. What does it mean to log-in a group or to pass it around for authentication?

These points argue against a COMPOSITE relationship between User and Group. But we still need an association between users and groups, because the system has to keep track of which users are in which groups.

In fact, for maximum performance we need a *two-way* mapping. It is likely that there will be many more users than groups. Therefore it must be possible to determine all the users in a group without examining every user in the system. Finding all the groups to which a user belongs is important too, as it makes checks for group membership fast.

An obvious way to implement a two-way mapping is by adding collections to the Group and Node classes: a collection of nodes to the Group class, and a collection of groups to the Node class. But there are two significant drawbacks to that approach:

1. The mapping is hard to change. We'd have to modify at least one and possibly two base classes.

2. All objects are saddled with the cost of the collection. Groups with no users still pay the cost of the collection, as do users not belonging to any group. At minimum, every object stores an extra pointer.

The mapping between groups and users is complex and potentially variable. The obvious approach distributes responsibility for the mapping and leads to the drawbacks I've mentioned. What is perhaps a less-obvious approach avoids these drawbacks by *centralizing* the responsibility.

The MEDIATOR pattern promotes object interaction to full object status. It fosters loose coupling by keeping objects from referring to each other explicitly, thereby letting you independently vary their interaction.

Here's the typical situation before applying the pattern. There's a set of interacting objects—the pattern refers to them generically as *colleagues*—each of which refers directly to (most) every other:

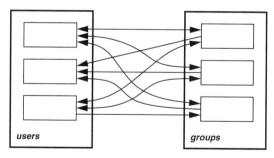

And here's the result of applying the pattern:

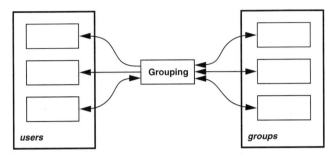

At the heart of the pattern is a Mediator object, which corresponds to the Grouping object in the second diagram. Instead of colleagues referring to each other explicitly, each refers to the mediator exclusively.

In our file system, the Grouping object defines a bidirectional mapping between users and groups. To make the mapping easy to change, the pattern employs an abstract base class for the Mediator object from which to derive mapping-specific subclasses. Here's a simple interface for the Grouping mediator that lets clients register and unregister associations between users and groups:

```
class Grouping {
public:
    virtual void ~Grouping();

    static const Grouping* getGrouping();
    static void setGrouping(
        const Grouping*, const User* = 0
    );

    virtual void register(
        const User*, const Group*, const User* = 0
    ) = 0;
    virtual void unregister(
        const User*, const Group*, const User* = 0
    ) = 0;

    virtual const Group* getGroup(
        const string& loginName, int index = 0
    ) = 0;
    virtual const string& getUser(
        const Group*, int index = 0
    ) = 0;
```

```
protected:
    Grouping();
    Grouping(const Grouping&);
};
```

The first thing to notice about this interface is the static `get` and `set` operations, which are analogous to those defined on User as a result of applying the SINGLETON pattern. I've applied that pattern here as well, and for the same reasons: The mapping needs to be globally accessible and settable.

By replacing the Grouping object at run-time, it's possible to change the mapping in one fell swoop. For example, a super-user might be able to redefine the mapping for administrative purposes. Changing the mapping should be a closely guarded operation, by the way, so the client must call `setGrouping` with an authorizing `const User*`. Similarly, the user supplied to the `register` and `unregister` operations must be authorized to make or break the mapping.

The last two operations, `getGroup` and `getUser`, identify associated group(s) and users(s). The optional `index` parameters give clients a simple way to step through multiple values. Concrete subclasses can define different implementations for these operations. Note that these operations do not deal with User objects directly but with strings for the corresponding login names. This lets any client see the associations without obtaining or supplying User objects it's not privy to.

One of MEDIATOR's pitfalls is the tendency toward monolithic Mediator classes. Because a Mediator encapsulates potentially complex interactions, it can become an unwieldy beast that's hard to maintain and extend. Applying other patterns can help guard against that eventuality. For example, you can use TEMPLATE METHOD to vary portions of a mediator's behavior in subclasses. STRATEGY lets you do the same thing with greater flexibility. COMPOSITE can let you compose a mediator out of smaller pieces through recursive composition.

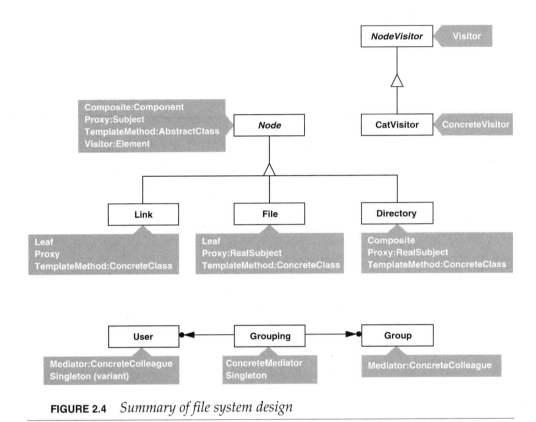

FIGURE 2.4 *Summary of file system design*

Wrapping Up

We have applied patterns to many aspects of our file system's design. COMPOSITE contributed the recursive tree structure that serves as the system's backbone. PROXY augmented that backbone with support for symbolic links. VISITOR gave us the wherewithal to add new, type-specific functionality gracefully and unintrusively.

As for protection, TEMPLATE METHOD provided it on a rudimentary level, that of individual operations. It was pretty much all we needed for single-user protection, but catering to multiple users called for additional abstractions—support for log-in, users, and groups. SIN-GLETON helped us at two levels: by encapsulating and controlling the sensitive log-in procedure, and by establishing an implicit user that can be accessed and replaced by any object in the system. Finally, MEDIATOR furnished a flexible and noninvasive way to associate users with the groups they're members of.

Figure 2.4 summarizes the patterns we've used and the classes that embody them. The notation is something Erich dreamed up a couple of years ago. He calls it "pattern:role annotation." It tags classes with shaded boxes containing any associated pattern(s) and/or participant name(s). For brevity, only the participant name is shown if the pattern is obvious and there's no ambiguity. By avoiding added lines and by using boxes with a contrasting background, clutter and interference are minimized—pattern annotations appear to occupy a different plane from the class structure. In fact, this notation actually *reduces* the number of lines because some notational artifacts are intrinsic to a pattern and can be omitted. Notice for example how I've omitted the aggregation relationship between Directory and Node, as it is intrinsic to the Component–Composite relationship in COMPOSITE.

I find Erich's notation highly readable, informative, and scalable, especially compared to my own Venn diagram-inspired notation (see Figure 2.3 on page 29). The only drawback I've seen is that the gray backgrounds don't fax too well. *Caveat scannor!*

CHAPTER 3

Themes and Variations

T his chapter presents new and improved insights on several of the original GoF patterns—SINGLETON, OBSERVER, VISITOR, and MEMENTO, to be exact—plus a brand new one, GENERATION GAP. The deliberations herein should convince you, in case you need convincing, that a pattern is never, *ever* finished.

To Kill a Singleton

The SINGLETON pattern is remarkably simple. Its Intent states,

> Ensure a class only has one instance, and provide a global point of access to it.

It's also flexible. In the file system design, SINGLETON helped us encapsulate the creation of User objects, which give file system users the authority to access their own files and no one else's. To obtain a User object, a client program calls a static User::logIn operation:

```
static const User* User::logIn(
    const string& loginName, const string& password
);
```

As you'll recall, this is just a gussied-up version of SINGLETON's static Instance operation. In the vanilla version of the pattern, Instance limits you to exactly one instance of the Singleton class (the User class in this case). But one of the pattern's consequences is the option to *control* the number of instances, as opposed to flatly precluding more than one. We availed ourselves of that option to preclude more than one User instance *per user*. That way, an application is free to create multiple instances if it caters to multiple users at the same time.

Another thing I brought up was the pattern's deafening silence on the issue of deletion. Who deletes Singleton instances, and how, and when? The words "delete" and "destructor" never appear in the pattern. Honest oversight? Conscious omission? Or perhaps evading a hard problem? I hope to convince you that it's neither of the last two. We'll also look at an assortment of new observations on this surprisingly rich little pattern.

Like any self-respecting class, a Singleton class should define a destructor. If Singleton is to be subclassed, then the destructor should be declared virtual. All just C++ 101. Now comes the tricky part: Should this destructor be public, private, or protected?

"What's the issue?" you might ask. "Make it public and get on with it." The implication here is that singleton destruction is *explicit*—that is, it's a client responsibility.

But there's a reasonable argument against that. The SINGLETON pattern places responsibility for object *creation* squarely in the Singleton class. Clients go to this class to get a Singleton instance. If a client deletes the instance without the Singleton class knowing about it, from then on the Singleton class will hand out "dangling references" that point to an object that no longer exists. Singleton's responsibilities imply that it *owns* the instance it creates; and ownership, finally, means responsibility for deletion. This is in contrast to other creational patterns, such as ABSTRACT FACTORY and FACTORY METHOD, that do not retain ownership of the instances they create.

That said, we might still get away with a public destructor *if* the following are true:

1. The destructor deletes and cleans up its references to the static instance. Then a subsequent call to the Instance operation will work as it did the first time.

2. Clients do not retain references to the Singleton object. Otherwise, they will be left with dangling references.

These restrictions are stringent enough to make explicit destruction the exception rather than the rule.

In our file system design, for example, we have to consider how and when User objects get deleted. Suppose we let clients delete User objects explicitly with the normal `delete` operator. We could be even more explicit and provide a static `logOut` operation that mirrors the `logIn` operation (whatever; the deletion interface doesn't really matter). Currently, however, there's no way for the User class to know which clients have references to User objects. So if a User gets deleted, clients may end up with dangling references—thoroughly unacceptable.

Although we probably need a mechanism for logging users out, say, for bookkeeping purposes, the potential for dangling references disqualifies deletion for the log-out mechanism. In other words, we shouldn't confuse logging out with deleting a User object. Regardless of which interface we choose for logging a user out, it cannot involve explicit destruction of a User object.

My point here is to make a case for rejecting the public destructor. Rejecting a *private* destructor is much easier—assuming we want to allow subclassing the Singleton class. That happens to be a bad assumption in our file system example; but in general, you do want to allow Singleton subclasses. That would leave only one choice—a protected destructor.

Back now to square one: How does a singleton ever get deleted?

The thing about Singleton objects is that they are usually, if not inherently, long-lived. Often they exist for the life of the program. You delete them not so much to reclaim space but to shut down in an orderly manner. You want to close files, unlock resources, terminate network connections, and so forth, without the appearance of an abrupt termination (read "crash"). If your Singleton objects ever need to do such cleanup, they probably have to wait until just before the program terminates. This is a nice property, because it means C++ may be able to do the deletion for us *implicitly.*

C++ deletes static objects automatically at program termination. The language guarantees that their destructors will be called and their space reclaimed, although it doesn't guarantee the calling order. For now let's assume that ordering isn't important; there is only one singleton in the program, or if there is more than one, their destruction is not order-dependent. That means we can define the Singleton class like this:

```
class Singleton {
public:
    static Singleton* instance();

protected:
    Singleton();
    Singleton(const Singleton&);

    friend class SingletonDestroyer;
    virtual ~Singleton() { }

private:
    static Singleton* _instance;
    static SingletonDestroyer _destroyer;
};

Singleton* Singleton::_instance = 0;
SingletonDestroyer Singleton::_destroyer;

Singleton* Singleton::instance () {
    if (!_instance) {
        _instance = new Singleton;
        _destroyer.setSingleton(_instance);
    }
    return _instance;
}
```

SingletonDestroyer is a class, the sole purpose of which is the destruction of a particular Singleton object:

```
class SingletonDestroyer {
public:
    SingletonDestroyer(Singleton* = 0);
    ~SingletonDestroyer();

    void setSingleton(Singleton* s);
    Singleton* getSingleton();
```

```
private:
    Singleton* _singleton;
};

SingletonDestroyer::SingletonDestroyer (Singleton* s) {
    _singleton = s;
}

SingletonDestroyer::~SingletonDestroyer () {
    delete _singleton;
}

void SingletonDestroyer::setSingleton (Singleton* s) {
    _singleton = s;
}

Singleton* SingletonDestroyer::getSingleton () {
    return _singleton;
}
```

The Singleton class declares a static SingletonDestroyer member, which gets created automatically at program start-up. If and when the user first calls Singleton::instance, not only will the Singleton object get created, but instance will also pass that object to the static SingletonDestroyer object, effectively transferring ownership to the SingletonDestroyer. When the program exits, the SingletonDestroyer is destroyed automagically, and the Singleton object along with it. Singleton destruction is now implicit.

Simple—almost. Note the friend in the declaration of the Singleton class. It's needed to give the destroyer access to Singleton's protected destructor. Not pretty if you have an aversion to the friend keyword, but it's necessary, given the earlier arguments against a public destructor. And it exemplifies what is perhaps the most defensible use of friend—to define another level of protection, as opposed to furnishing a work-around to a bad design.

To maximize reuse, especially if there are multiple kinds of singletons in your program, you might save yourself some typing and define a templatized Destroyer class:[1]

---

1. Followers of the standardization process will recognize this as the standard library's auto_ptr class template, coming soon to a programming environment near you.

```
template <class DOOMED>
class Destroyer {
public:
    Destroyer(DOOMED* = 0);
    ~Destroyer();

    void setDoomed(DOOMED*);
    DOOMED* getDoomed();
private:
    // Prevent users from making copies of a
    // Destroyer to avoid double deletion:
    Destroyer(const Destroyer<DOOMED>&);
    void operator=(const Destroyer<DOOMED>&);
private:
    DOOMED* _doomed;
};
template <class DOOMED>
Destroyer<DOOMED>::Destroyer (DOOMED* d) {
    _doomed = d;
}
template <class DOOMED>
Destroyer<DOOMED>::~Destroyer () {
    delete _doomed;
}
template <class DOOMED>
void Destroyer<DOOMED>::setDoomed (DOOMED* d) {
    _doomed = d;
}
template <class DOOMED>
DOOMED* Destroyer<DOOMED>::getDoomed () {
    return _doomed;
}
```

That lets us define Singleton like this:

```
class Singleton {
public:
    static Singleton* instance();

protected:
    Singleton();
    Singleton(const Singleton&);
```

```
    friend class Destroyer<Singleton>;
    virtual ~Singleton() { }
private:
    static Destroyer<Singleton> _destroyer;
};

Destroyer<Singleton> Singleton::_destroyer;

Singleton* Singleton::instance () {
    if (!_instance) {
        _instance = new Singleton;
        _destroyer.setDoomed(_instance);
    }
    return _instance;
}
```

There are two potential problems with implicit destruction. First, it doesn't help you if you need to delete your singleton *before* the end of the program. In that case, it's hard to imagine an approach that doesn't require explicit destruction. Moreover, you'll either have to add mechanism (say, reference-counting) to minimize the dangling reference problem, or you'll have to force clients to access the Singleton instance exclusively through the Singleton::instance operation.

One way to do the latter involves (1) making instance return a reference to a Singleton and (2) disallowing copy and initialization by declaring the assignment and copy constructors private:

```
class Singleton {
public:
    static Singleton& instance();

protected:
    // ...

private:
    Singleton(const Singleton&);
    Singleton& operator=(const Singleton&);
    // ...
};
```

This approach isn't foolproof, unfortunately, because a client can always take the address of the value that instance returns, or it can cast away these safeguards entirely. Nevertheless, this issue is unlikely to be a show-stopper. As I pointed out earlier, the SINGLETON pattern favors long-lived objects, so explicit deletion probably won't be a common problem.

The second and thornier problem surfaces when you've got multiple Singleton objects in your program, and they depend on each other. In that case, the order of destruction might be significant.

Consider our file system design, where we applied the SINGLETON pattern twice. We used it first to control the number of User objects, which produced the singleton User class. The second application ensured just one Grouping object, which defines a mapping between users and the groups they belong to. The Grouping object lets us define protection for groups of users rather than just individuals. Because it doesn't make sense (in fact it's downright dangerous) to have more than one grouping active at once, we made the Grouping class a Singleton.

A Grouping object maintains references to both User objects and Group objects. It doesn't own the User objects, but it could conceivably own the Group objects. In any case, it seems to me desirable to delete the Grouping object *before* the User objects, rugged individualist that I am. True, the dangling references that would otherwise result probably won't be a problem, since Grouping shouldn't have to dereference any of them during its destruction. Then again, you never know.

My point is simply this: The destroyer approach, based as it is on an unspecified language implementation mechanism, begins to fray when destruction order is important. If your application calls for multiple, dependent singletons, then you may have to revert to explicit destruction. One thing's for sure: You can't use more than one destroyer if the Singleton destructors depend on one another.

An alternative is to eschew destroyers altogether and rely instead on the draft-standard `atexit()` function, as Tim Peierls suggested to me [Peierls96]:

> I maintain that `atexit()` is a good way to clean up singletons in C++ when you really want single instances with program lifetime and no replacement. The draft standard promises a lot:
>
>> §3.6.3, paragraph 1: The function `atexit()` from `<cstdlib>` can be used to specify a function to be called at exit. If `atexit()` is to be called, the implementation shall not destroy objects initialized before an `atexit()` call until after the function specified in the `atexit()` call has been called.

The only way I can see this failing is if a statically initialized object whose destructor depends on a Singleton instance is initialized after the Singleton instance is constructed, that is, through some other static initialization. This suggests that classes [having static instances] should avoid depending on singletons during destruction. (Or at least there should be a way for such classes to check for the existence of the Singleton during destruction.)

Even though this obviates the need for destroyers, the real problem— deleting mutually dependent singletons—remains. Garbage collection, anyone?

Long ago, in a galaxy far, far away, Scott Meyers posited the following [Meyers95]:

> My [version of SINGLETON] is quite similar to yours, but instead of using a class static and having `instance` return a pointer, I use a function static and return a reference:
>
> ```
> Singleton& Singleton::instance () {
>     static Singleton s;
>     return s;
> }
> ```
>
> This seems to offer every advantage your solution does (no construction if never used, no dependence on initialization order between translation units, etc.), plus it allows users to use object syntax instead of pointer syntax. Furthermore, my solution makes it much less likely a caller will inadvertently delete the singleton in a misguided attempt to avoid a memory leak.
>
> Am I overlooking a reason for returning a pointer to a class static instead of a reference to a function static?

The only drawback I could see here is that a function static makes it hard to extend the Singleton through subclassing, since `instance` always creates an object of type Singleton. (For more on extending the Singleton class, see the discussion beginning on page 130 in *Design Patterns*.) At any rate, one needn't worry about deleting the Singleton instance if its destructor isn't public. While I have since developed a slight preference for returning a reference, in the end it seems to make little difference—in single-threaded applications, that is.

Later, Erich Gamma noticed a more fundamental difficulty with Scott's proposal [Gamma95]:

> It turns out that it is not possible to make [Scott's approach] thread-safe if multiple threads can call `instance`. The problem is that [some C++ compilers generate] internal data structures that cannot be protected by locks. In such situations you would have to acquire the lock at the call site—pretty ugly.

Yep. And it wouldn't be long before Doug Schmidt got bitten by a related and even more fundamental bug [Schmidt96b]:

> [The Double-Checked Locking] pattern [SH98] emerged as I was proof-reading John Vlissides' Pattern Hatching column for April '96. In this column, John talks about SINGLETON in the context of protection for multiuser file systems. Ironically, we'd been having some mysterious problems recently with memory leaks on multithreaded versions of ACE on multiprocessors.
>
> As I read John's column, it suddenly struck me that the problem was caused by multiply initialized Singletons due to race conditions. Once I saw the connection between the two issues, and factored in the key forces (e.g., no locking overhead for normal use of the Singleton), the solution jumped right out.

About a month later, Doug sent me a follow-up [Schmidt96c]:

> [O]ne of my grad students (Tim Harrison) recently implemented a C++ library class called Singleton, which basically adapts existing classes to become "Singletons." We use this in ACE now, and it's quasi-useful. The nice thing about it is that it automates the [Double-Checked locking pattern] and also enables easy parameterization of the LOCK strategy. I've enclosed it below, just for fun.

```
template <class TYPE, class LOCK>
class Singleton {
public:
    static TYPE* instance();

protected:
    static TYPE* _instance;
    static LOCK _lock;
};
```

```
template <class TYPE, class LOCK>
TYPE* Singleton<TYPE, LOCK>::instance () {
    // perform the Double-Check pattern...

    if (_instance == 0) {
        Guard<LOCK> monitor(_lock);

        if (_instance == 0) _instance = new TYPE;
    }

    return _instance;
}
```

I was intrigued, especially the part about being "quasi-useful." I asked whether he said that because this approach doesn't really preclude creating multiple objects of the base type (since presumably that type is defined as a non-singleton elsewhere). His response was illuminating, and a little unnerving [Schmidt96d]:

Right, exactly. Another problem is that many C++ compilers (e.g., g++) don't implement static data members within templates. In this case you have to implement the static instance method like this:

```
template <class TYPE, class LOCK>
TYPE* Singleton<TYPE, LOCK>::instance () {
    static TYPE* _instance = 0;
    static LOCK _lock;

    if (_instance == 0)
    // ...

    return _instance;
}
```

Ah, the joys of cross-platform C++ portability! ;-)

That, in turn, fired a few dormant neurons. I wrote back that if you really wanted to make a class inherently Singleton, you could subclass it from this template, passing the subclass as a template parameter (Cope's curiously recurring template pattern again [Coplien95]—I love it!). For example:

```
class User : public Singleton<User, Mutex> { ... }
```

That way, you would preserve Singleton semantics without recoding the pattern in all its multithreaded gory (*sic*).

Caution: I haven't tried out this variation myself, nor have I had occasion to use it. I just think it's neat, both aesthetically and in the way we arrived at it. I used to think SINGLETON was one of the more trivial of our patterns, hardly worthy to hobnob with the likes of COMPOSITE, VISITOR, etc.; and maybe that attitude explains its silence on some issues. Boy, was I wrong.

The Trouble with OBSERVER

The software industry is notorious for its disclaimers. Developers can pretty much disavow any and all responsibility for their creations. So in the spirit of equal access,

> WARNING: This section contains speculative designs that are provided on an "as-is" basis. The author and publisher make no warranty of any kind, expressed or implied, regarding these designs. But feel free to bet your career on them anyway.

What I'm doing here is thinking aloud about a design problem that's nettled me for almost a decade now, because the common cure is often worse than the disease.

Suppose you're building a framework for business applications, which manipulate primitive data such as dollar amounts, names, addresses, percentages, and the like. They present this data through one or more user interfaces: fixed text for unchanging alphanumeric data; a text entry field for editable data; buttons, sliders, or pop-up menus for more constrained inputs; visual presentations such as pie charts, bar graphs, and plots of different sorts—you get the idea.

You decide that it's important to keep changes to the user interface from interfering with application functionality and vice versa. So you separate the user interface from the underlying application data. In fact, you consider a full-blown Smalltalk Model-View-Controller (MVC)-like partitioning between the two [KP88]. MVC not only separates the application data from the user interface but also allows multiple user interfaces to the same data.

Thumbing through *Design Patterns*, you spy the OBSERVER pattern, which tells you how to achieve this partitioning. OBSERVER captures the relationship between the primitive data and its potentially numerous presentations, as follows:

1. Each piece of data is encapsulated in a Subject object (corresponding to a model in MVC).

2. Each distinct user interface to a subject is encapsulated in an Observer object (corresponding to a view in MVC).

3. A subject can have multiple observers at once.

4. Whenever the subject changes, it notifies its observer(s) of the change.

5. In turn, the observers query their subject for information that impacts their appearance; then they update themselves appropriately.

The subject stores the definitive information, and observers get updated whenever the subject's information changes. When the user saves his or her work, it is the subject that gets saved; the observers needn't be saved because the information they display comes from their subject.

Here's an example. To let a user change a numerical value, such as an interest rate, an application might provide a text entry field and a pair of up–down buttons, as shown in Figure 3.1. When the subject that stores the interest rate changes (say, because a user increased the interest rate a notch by pressing the up button), it notifies its observer—the text entry field. In response, the text entry field redisplays itself to reflect the new interest rate.

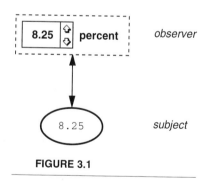

FIGURE 3.1

Now, in addition to primitive data, the applications that use our framework need higher-order abstractions such as loans, contracts, business partners, and products. To maximize reuse, you want to compose these abstractions out of fine-grained subjects and observers.

Take a look at Figure 3.2, which shows a user interface for entering loan information. The interface is implemented as an observer of a subject. Figure 3.3 shows that this observer is actually a *composition* of primitive observers, and that the subject is a composition of the corresponding primitive subjects.

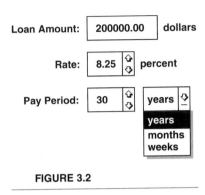

FIGURE 3.2

This design has four nice properties:

1. You can define, modify, and extend subjects independently of observers, and vice versa—a boon to maintenance and enhancement.

2. Your application can include only the functionality it needs. This is particularly important when the framework offers lots of functionality. If, for example, an application doesn't need to present application data graphically, then it needn't include observers that present pie charts or bar graphs. It's strictly pay-as-you-go.

3. You can attach any number of observers to the same subject. The text entry field and up–down buttons would likely be implemented as separate observers. (I didn't show this in the figures to

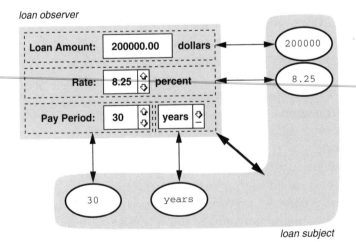

FIGURE 3.3 *Loan subject and observer compositions*

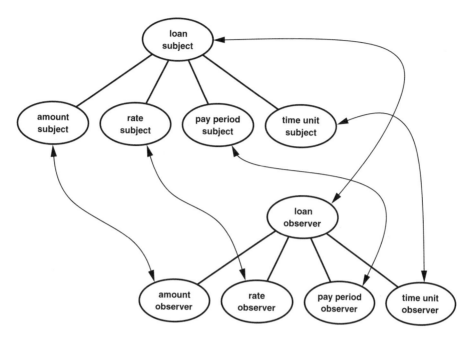

FIGURE 3.4 *Loan subject and observer object structures*

keep them simple.) You can even have nonvisual observers. For example, you can define an object that logs changes to a subject's data without modifying the subject's implementation.

4. You can implement new subjects and observers in terms of existing ones, promoting reuse.

Sounds wonderful, and it is. Alas, there is a dark side.

Figure 3.4 shows another way to look at these object compositions: as containment hierarchies. The loan subject contains its primitive constituents, and the loan observer contains corresponding primitive observers. Note the abundance of objects (*labeled ovals*) and object references (*lines*). There are links between not only the loan subject and loan observer but also between each primitive subject and its observer.

In short, the OBSERVER pattern has produced a lot of redundancy at run-time. If you were coding the loan subject and loan observer from scratch, you could easily eliminate most of these links, not to mention many of the objects themselves. They're all included in the price we pay for reuse.

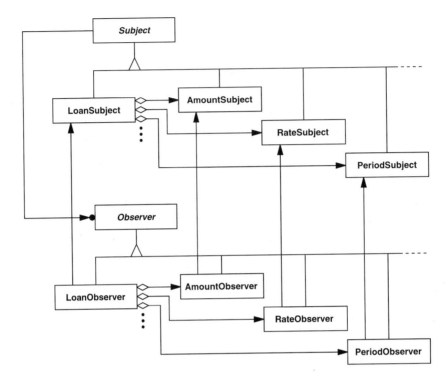

FIGURE 3.5 *Loan subject and observer class structures*

But wait—there's more! Run-time redundancy is only part of the problem; we've got static redundancy too. Consider the classes that implement these object structures. OBSERVER prescribes separate Subject and Observer class hierarchies wherein the abstract base classes define the notification protocol and the interface for attaching and detaching observers. ConcreteSubject subclasses implement specific subjects, adding whatever interface their concrete observers need to figure out what changed. Meanwhile ConcreteObserver subclasses define distinct presentations of their subjects, with their Update operation specifying how they update themselves.

Figure 3.5 summarizes these static relationships. Pretty complicated, huh? Parallel hierarchies tend to get that way. Beyond the mechanical overhead of coding and maintaining these hierarchies, there's also conceptual overhead. Programmers have to understand twice as many classes, twice as many interfaces, and twice as many subclassing issues.

Wouldn't it be *more* wonderful if we could get away with just one class hierarchy and one instance hierarchy? Trouble is, we don't want to give up the clean partitioning of application data and user interface that separate class and object hierarchies buy us. What to do?

Think for a minute. A major run-time cost of the subject–observer split is—what? Surely it's the memory overhead of collateral objects and links. Parallel object hierarchies require double the number of objects and intra-hierarchy links, in addition to links *between* the hierarchies. That's a lot of information to keep lying around. In fact, we should question how necessary all this is. Do we really access the information so very often? It's one thing to separate user interface from application data, but must we constantly maintain scads of links between the two?

Assuming these questions are loaded and the answer to both is No, then what's an alternative? Limiting ourselves to one object hierarchy is a sure way to cut down on both objects and links. The trick is to retain the benefits of redundancy. We've got to find a way to present subject information without maintaining a parallel observer hierarchy and without simply lumping the hierarchies together.

Since memory is an issue here, let's contemplate a classic trade-off between space and time. Instead of *storing* the information, how about *computing* it on the fly? We don't have to store information we can recreate on demand—provided we don't demand it very often. How often is "very often"? Often enough to have a unacceptable impact on performance.

Fortunately, the number of situations in which observers actually do anything is pretty small, at least in our application. Basically they spring to life in three circumstances:

1. When the subject changes.
2. When there's user input.
3. When (part of) the user interface must be (re)drawn.

These circumstances constitute the times observer code would execute. If we eliminate the observer objects, then these are the times we'll have to figure out what to do on the fly.

Don't get me wrong. I'm not saying we won't use *any* objects to do the observers' work. We'll use objects all right; we just want to use substantially fewer of them than OBSERVER calls for—hopefully a constant number, as opposed to a number proportional to the size of the subject hierarchy. We don't want to store a zillion links to subjects either. We'd like to compute the links rather than store them.

The three circumstances I've described usually precipitate traversal(s) of the observer structure or the subject structure (and often both). A change to a subject and the resulting change to its observer may necessitate a traversal of the entire observer structure, for example, to redraw affected user interface elements. Similarly, the computation that determines which user interface element got clicked involves at least a partial traversal of the observer structure. Ditto for redrawing.

Since we're likely to do a traversal under any of these circumstances, traversal might be a splendid time to compute what we would have otherwise stored. As a matter of fact, traversal can provide enough context to do things that would be impossible for subjects to do unilaterally.

For example, we could update a modified subject's appearance by traversing the subject structure and redrawing the user interface in its entirety. No doubt such a simple-minded approach is less efficient than we'd like, because presumably only a small part of the user interface needs to change. Fortunately, the remedy is equally simple-minded: Just have subjects maintain a "dirty bit"[2] that indicates whether they've changed. Their dirty bits get reset as a side-effect of traversal. Hence we can ignore all but the dirty subjects during traversal, bringing the efficiency of this approach more in line with OBSERVER's.

"Hey," one could rightly interject at this point, "How the heck do we know what to do at each step in the traversal?" And, "Where is that knowledge implemented?"

When we had Observer objects, each one knew how to draw its piece of the presentation. The code for presenting a particular ConcreteSubject lived in a corresponding ConcreteObserver class. The subject ended up delegating its presentation to its observer(s). It's this delegation that led to lots of additional objects and references.

---

2. The implementation should be hidden behind a set/get interface, so the actual amount of storage can vary.

Having rid ourselves of observers, we need a new place to put the presentation code for a subject. We must assume the presentation is drawn incrementally (subject-by-subject) during traversal, and we must vary the presentation according to the type of subject. The code that gets executed at each point in the traversal depends on two things: the kind of subject and the kind of presentation. If all we have is a subject hierarchy, how do we tell the subjects apart, and how does the correct code get executed?

Ambiguities like these result from removing presentation functionality from the subject. But we don't want to retreat to a lumped subject and observer, nor do we want to resort to unseemly run-time type tests if we can help it.

VISITOR *Revisited*

We've had a problem like this before, back in Chapter 2 to be exact, when we were in the thick of designing a file system. There were lots of different things we wanted file system objects (e.g., files and directories) to be able to do. But we didn't want to keep adding operations to Node—the abstract base class for file system objects. Each new operation would require surgery to existing code, heightening the risk of K-S[3] syndrome in the Node interface.

That's when I introduced the VISITOR pattern. New functionality got implemented in separate Visitor objects, obviating the need to change the Node base class. The key thing about visitors is that they recover type information from the objects they visit. For example, we can define a Visitor class called `Presenter` that does everything needed to present a given subject, including drawing, input handling, and so forth. Its interface might look like this:

```
class Presenter {
public:
    Presenter();

    virtual void visit(LoanSubject*);
    virtual void visit(AmountSubject*);
    virtual void visit(RateSubject*);
```

---

3. Kitchen-Sink

```
        virtual void visit(PeriodSubject*);
        // visit operations for other ConcreteSubjects

        virtual void init(Subject*);
        virtual void draw(Window*, Subject*);
        virtual void redraw(Window*, Subject*);
        virtual void handle(Event*, Subject*);
        // other operations involving traversal
};
```

You'll recall that VISITOR requires an accept operation of every kind of object that can be visited. These operations are all implemented the same way. For example:

```
void LoanSubject::accept (Presenter& p) {
    p.visit(this);
}
```

To generate a presentation of a given subject, each stage of the traversal calls subject->accept(p), in which subject is of type Subject*, and p is an instance of Presenter. Herein lies the magic of VISITOR: The call back on the presenter resolves statically to the correct subclass-specific Presenter operation, effectively identifying the concrete subject to the presenter—run-time type tests need not apply.

If you're wondering who carries out the traversal, look again at Presenter's interface: It includes init, draw, redraw, and handle—operations over and above what VISITOR prescribes. These operations carry out one or more traversals in response to a stimulus such as a user input, a change in subject state, or any other traversal-prompting circumstance described earlier. These operations give clients a simple interface for keeping the presentation alive and up-to-date. Figure 3.6 graphically depicts the traversal process. Compare the number of objects and links (*solid lines*) to that of Figure 3.4 on page 75. A substantial reduction, no?

VISITOR aficionados know all too well how the pattern falls down when the class structure you visit isn't stable, and that weakness bodes ill for our business application framework. Ideally, our repertoire of Subject subclasses is comprehensive enough so that programmers would never have to define their own subclasses. But our world isn't exactly ideal, and it must be possible (if not easy) to define presentations for new Subject subclasses without changing the framework. In particular, we don't want to have to add new visit operations to the Presenter class in support of new Subject subclasses.

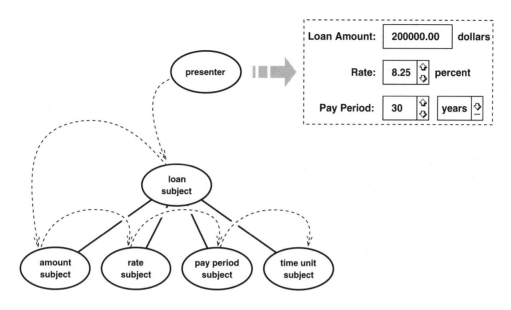

FIGURE 3.6   *Presenter traversal*

Back in Chapter 2 I introduced a catch-all `visit` operation into the Visitor interface (page 36) as a place to implement default behavior. Doing the same here would entail adding

```
virtual void visit(Subject*);
```

to the Presenter interface. If there is default behavior that all `visit` operations should implement, you can put it in `visit(Subject*)` and have the other `visit` operations call it by default. That way you avoid duplicating default functionality.

But this catch-all operation offers more than just occasional reuse. It provides a veritable trap door through which to visit unforeseen Subject subclasses.

Suppose I'm an application programmer (which I am), and I've just defined a new RebateSubject subclass of Subject. I've dutifully implemented its `accept` operation the same as all the others:

```
void RebateSubject::accept (Presenter& p) {
    p.visit(this);
}
```

If you didn't understand why the catch-all operation is important, then this scenario should make it clear. When `RebateSubject::accept` calls `visit` with itself as an argument, the compiler must find a corresponding operation in the Presenter interface. If there were no `Presenter::visit(Subject*)` as a catch-all, the compiler would throw up its hands and spit out an error message. Not so with the catch-all. The compiler is smart enough to know that a RebateSubject is a Subject, and everything's hunky-dory as far as type compatibility goes.

But while we've sated the compiler, we haven't accomplished much. `Presenter::visit(Subject*)` was implemented before there ever was a RebateSubject class. That means it can't do anything beyond the default behavior it implements, which is probably no behavior at all.

What now?

Recall what we're trying to avoid: the need to change the Visitor (that is, Presenter) interface. And why? Because the application programmer cannot change an interface defined by the framework. However, nothing prevents the programmer from *subclassing* Presenter. That's exactly how we'll add code for presenting RebateSubjects.

Let's define a NewPresenter subclass. Beyond the Presenter functionality it inherits, it adds code for presenting RebateSubjects by overriding the catch-all operation:[4]

```
void NewPresenter::visit (Subject* s) {
    RebateSubject* rs = dynamic_cast<RebateSubject*>(s);

    if (rs) {
        // present the RebateSubject
    } else {
        Presenter::visit(s); // carry out default behavior
    }
}
```

Now you see the dirty little secret of this approach: the run-time type test to ensure that the subject we're visiting is in fact a RebateSub-

---

4. A C++ quirk: Because I've overloaded the `visit` operations, we must override *all* of them in `NewPresenter` to head off complaints from the compiler. To avoid this problem, forgo overloading and embed the concrete subject's name in the `visit` operation, or use `using` as Kevlin Henney suggests (see page 37). I discuss this problem more fully a bit earlier, beginning on page 35.

ject. If we were absolutely sure that `NewPresenter::visit(Subject*)` could be called only by visiting a RebateSubject, then we could replace the dynamic cast with a static cast. That's a dicey thing to do nevertheless. Besides, you'll *have* to do the dynamic cast if there's more than one new subclass of Subject to visit and present.

Obviously this is meant to work around a drawback of the VISITOR pattern. If you're constantly adding new Subject subclasses, then the whole VISITOR approach degrades into a tag-and-case-statement style of programming. But when applications define just a few new subclasses, as should be the case in a design that favors composition, then most of the benefits of the VISITOR pattern are retained.

The hopelessly analytical among you are wondering why I put the downcast in the `visit` operation when I could have put it in `RebateSubject::accept`, like so:

```
void RebateSubject::accept (Presenter& p) {
    NewPresenter* np = dynamic_cast<NewPresenter*>(&p);

    if (np) {
        np->visit(this);
    } else {
        Subject::accept(p); // carry out default behavior
    }
}
```

Turns out this works equally well in the short term, but it's harder to maintain. There may come a time when we've defined a critical mass of new Subject subclasses. At that point we're prepared to bite the bullet and change `Presenter` to add `visit` operations for heretofore unsupported subclasses like `RebateSubject`. Then the Presenter interface will once again reflect all the classes that a presenter can visit, and we can flush all the downcasting hocus-pocus.

Now think about what that would entail if we've been putting the downcasts in the new ConcreteVisitors' `visit` operations. We'd have to change the Presenter class, of course, and we should remove the downcasts from operations like `NewPresenter::visit(Subject*)`. But that's it—changes are confined to one class hierarchy. We won't have to touch the Subject hierarchy, because all the `accept` operations there are fine as they are. For example,

```
void RebateSubject::accept (Presenter& p) {
    p.visit(this);
}
```

still compiles happily, only now the `visit` call resolves statically to the newly added `Presenter::visit(RebateSubject*)`.[5]

If on the other hand we've been putting the downcasts in the `accept` operations, there's more to do: Each `accept` must be changed to look like the previous RebateSubject's. That's clearly undesirable, because a strong motivation for applying VISITOR in the first place is to avoid changes to the Element hierarchy you're visiting.

Again, if you're constantly defining Element subclasses, you shouldn't be applying VISITOR. But even when you're not defining them, prudence calls for at least *allowing* new subclasses, unless there's good reason not to. Hence the need for a catch-all. When you provide one, be sure to put your downcasts there, and overload the `visit` operations if at all possible.

There are still a few problems with this VISITOR-based alternative to OBSERVER. The first problem has to do with the size of our Presenter class. We have lumped the functionality of several ConcreteObserver classes into this one Visitor, and we don't want the result to be a huge monolith. At some point, we should start decomposing Presenter into smaller Visitors, perhaps by applying other patterns to reduce its size. For example, we could use STRATEGY to let `visit` operations delegate their work to Strategy objects. You'll recall, however, that one of the reasons we applied VISITOR in the first place was to reduce the number of objects we use. Putting more objects into the Visitor diminishes the

---

5. Note that if we hadn't overloaded `visit`—that is, if the type of subject being visited were embedded in the `visit` operation's name—then we would have to go back and change `accept` after all. That's because the `accept` of every new Subject subclass calls the catch-all operation explicitly:

```
void RebateSubject::accept (Presenter& p) {
    p.visitSubject(this);
}
```

This is reason enough to use overloading if your language supports it.

pattern's benefit. Still, it's unlikely we'll end up with as many objects (and links) as OBSERVER requires.

Another problem involves observer state. Nominally, the VISITOR approach has replaced lots of observers with one visitor. But what if each observer stores its own distinct state, not all of which is computable on the fly—where does that state end up? Because we've presumed that we can compute observer state rather than store it, this shouldn't be an issue. Worse comes to worst, if the uncomputable state truly varies on a per-object basis, then the visitor can keep that state in a private associative store (e.g., a hash table) keyed by subject. The difference in run-time overhead between the hash table and OBSERVER implementations should be negligible (he says).

All right, maybe this whole thing sounds a little hare-brained, and I'm not promising it isn't. The nice thing about paper designs is that they don't have to compile and run and ultimately put food on the table. But if there's even a germ of a useful idea here, please take advantage of it. If it turns out there isn't—or worse—well, that's what disclaimers are for!

GENERATION GAP

I wish I had a nickel for every time I've been asked, "When will you guys publish a second volume of patterns?" It hasn't helped that *Design Patterns* mentions how "a couple of patterns got dropped" from its repertoire "because they didn't seem important enough." Actually, we mothballed at least half a dozen patterns over the years, for reasons ranging from "doesn't seem important enough," to "not enough known uses," to "this sucker is hopeless."

GENERATION GAP is one of those that had languished for lack of known uses. I eventually published it anyway [Vlissides96], noting this shortcoming and making a public appeal for more examples. I got several responses, which I include here in this updated incarnation.

Pattern Name

Generation Gap

Classification

Class Structural

Intent

Modify or extend generated code just once no matter how many times it is regenerated.

Motivation

Having a computer generate code for you is usually preferable to writing it yourself, *provided* the code it generates is

- Correct
- Efficient enough
- Functionally complete
- Maintainable

Many code generation tools (such as user interface builders, parser generators, "wizards," and 4GL compilers) have no problem generating code that's correct and efficient. In fact, people have been known to study computer-generated code in preference to voluminous documentation in the course of learning a new programming interface. But generating *functionally complete and maintainable* code is another story.

Normally, you can't create a finished, nontrivial application automatically with one of these tools; you have to implement some functionality the old-fashioned way, by hand, in a programming language. That's because the high-level metaphor that gives the tool its power is rarely expressive enough to specify every (not-so-)little detail. The tool's abstractions are necessarily different from those of the programming language. The resulting mixed metaphor can wreak havoc on the application's extensibility and maintainability.

Consider a user interface builder that lets you assemble not only user interface elements, such as buttons, scroll bars, and menus (a.k.a. "widgets"), but also more primitive graphical objects such as

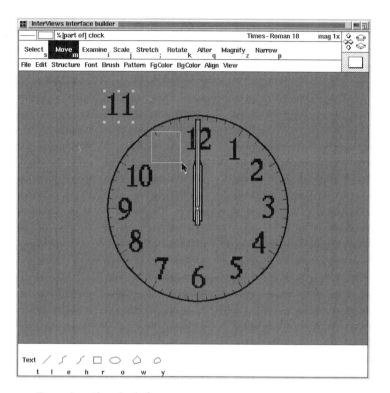

FIGURE 3.7 *Drawing the clock face*

lines, circles, polygons, and text.[6] The builder lets you draw pictures with these objects and then associate behavior with them. Hence you can specify more of the application in the tool than would be possible if it provided widgets alone.

You can use such a builder to create the complete user interface for an alarm clock application. You can draw the clock face by assembling lines, polygons, and text as shown in Figure 3.7. Then you add buttons for setting the current time, the alarm time, and for shutting off the alarm. The builder lets you compose all these elements into a complete user interface for the application.

What the builder doesn't let you specify, however, is how these elements behave when the application runs. Specifically, you need to

6. An example of such a builder is *ibuild*, part of the InterViews toolkit [VT91].

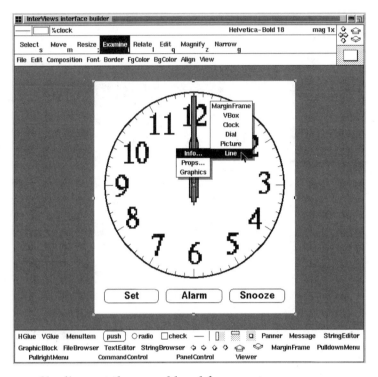

FIGURE 3.8   *Singling out the second hand for export*

program the behavior of the buttons and the hour, minute, and second hands. The most basic thing you need to be able to do is refer to these objects in your code. This builder lets you single out objects for "export"—that is, you can give them names by which to refer to them programmatically. In Figure 3.8, the user is singling out the second hand, an instance of a Line class, for export. The builder pops up a dialog box in response (Figure 3.9), letting you type in an evocative name like _sec_hand for the Line instance.

The builder can create other elements of the clock's user interface, such as the dialog boxes that let a user specify the current time and the alarm time. When you've finished the interface, the builder generates code that assembles the graphical components and lays them out as specified. It also assembles the dialog boxes and implements default actions for all the buttons. But like most application builders, that's about all this tool can do for you. You must revert to programming to

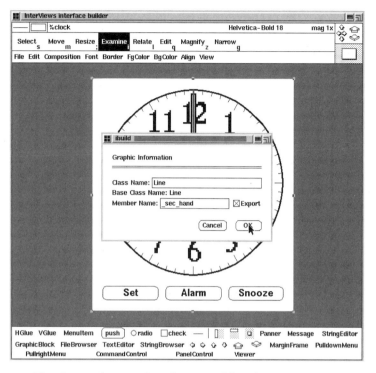

FIGURE 3.9 *Naming and exporting the second hand*

specify what the buttons really do when they're pressed, how the clock keeps time, and how it maintains the proper appearance. Most behavior remains to be programmed manually. How do you do it?

In the most straightforward approach, you'd take the code the builder generates and change it to suit your needs. For example, you would add code that generates an event of some sort every second. You'd also write a corresponding event handler that would rotate the second hand and possibly the minute and hour hands by appropriate amounts every second (minus 6° for the second hand).[7] Still more new code would implement button behavior. You continue changing the generated code by hand until you wind up with a working application.

---

7. Presumably, lines and other graphical objects have an interface for rotating themselves by a given angle.

Now for the maintenance problem. Suppose you want to rearrange the user interface so that the buttons appear *above* the clock face instead of below it. In other words, you want to change just the appearance, not the behavior. Any builder worth its salt will make cosmetic changes like this easy. Trouble is, the builder knows nothing about your modifications to the code it generated earlier. Regenerating the code blindly will clobber your changes, or at least will force you to reapply them.

There are several approaches to this problem. The builder can mark the code it generates as user-modifiable or not, usually by annotating it with dire warnings against modification. But that approach is unsatisfactory for at least two reasons:

1. *It's messy.* Although an improvement over ad hoc modification, hand-programmed code still mingles with the generated code. The result looks cluttered at best, to the extent that people may turn to tools to make it more readable—by hiding or highlighting different parts on demand, for example. Tools seldom mask such problems completely, however.

2. *It's error-prone.* Because modifications are governed solely by convention, the compiler can't check for illegal changes. If you make a mistake and modify the wrong code, the generator may blow away your changes later.

A more sophisticated approach computes the differences between the modified code and the code generated originally, and then attempts to merge differences into the regenerated code. Needless to say, this is a dicey proposition when the hand modifications are extensive—or sometimes just nontrivial.

An ideal solution would be more reliable than that, and for maintainability's sake it would keep generated code separate from hand-programmed modifications. But a strict separation can be hard to achieve, because modifications often need to access parts of the generated code that should not be public. For example, the Line object representing the second hand probably shouldn't be accessible to objects outside the clock, because the line is an implementation artifact. Even a higher-level interface for advancing the second hand probably shouldn't be made public—after all, most real-life clocks have no such capability.

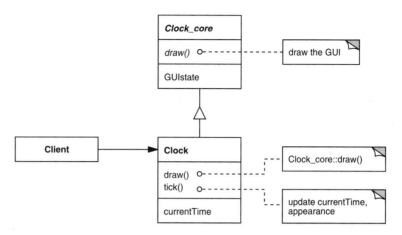

FIGURE 3.10 *Extending the core class*

GENERATION GAP is a pattern that solves this problem through class inheritance. It encapsulates generated code in a base class and modifications in a corresponding subclass.

In our clock example, the builder would encapsulate the code it generates in a **core class** named Clock_core. All the code that implements the clock as specified in the builder—including the graphical objects, widgets, and the way they are composed—lives in this class. No one ever instantiates the core class. Rather, the class to instantiate is the Clock class, also known generically as the **extension class**. The builder generates the extension class along with the core class.

As the name "extension class" suggests, Clock is a subclass of Clock_core. But it's a *trivial* subclass: It neither adds, removes, nor modifies state or behavior of the core class. It does nothing more or less than its superclass. Nevertheless, code that creates Clock objects *always* instantiates Clock, the extension class—not Clock_core, the core class.

So where do modifications go? You could modify the core class to work with other application code, but subsequent editing in the builder and regeneration would result in the code merging problem described earlier. Instead, you modify the *extension* class—never the core class—to add, change, or remove functionality. You can define new member functions, and you can redefine or extend the core class virtual functions (Figure 3.10). By declaring exported instances as protected member variables in C++, the extension class can access them without exposing them to clients.

If you want to modify the interface's appearance later, then the builder can regenerate *only* the core class, which you haven't modified; your original changes to the extension class are thus unaffected. Then recompile the application, and it will reflect the change in appearance. Only if you make radical changes to the interface (like removing the second hand or any other instances to which modifications refer) should you have to amend your original changes.

Applicability

Apply GENERATION GAP when *all* of the following are true:

- Code is generated automatically.
- Generated code can be encapsulated in one or more classes.
- Regenerated code usually retains the interface and instance variables of the previous generation.
- Generated classes usually aren't integrated into existing class hierarchies. If they are and your implementation language does not support multiple interface inheritance, then the code generator must allow you to specify the superclass of any base class it generates.

Structure

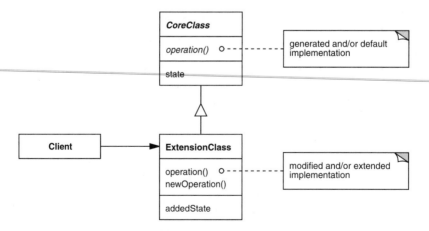

Participants

CoreClass (Clock_core)

- an abstract class containing a tool-generated implementation.
- is never modified by hand.
- is overwritten by the tool on regeneration.

ExtensionClass (Clock)

- a trivial subclass of CoreClass.
- implements extensions of or modifications to CoreClass. A programmer may change ExtensionClass to add state and/or extend, modify, or override CoreClass behavior.
- preserves extensions and modifications across regenerations.

Client

- instantiates and refers to ExtensionClass only.

Collaborations

- ExtensionClass inherits tool-generated behavior from CoreClass, overriding or extending its behavior.
- CoreClass exposes and/or delegates select functionality to ExtensionClass to allow modification or extension of its behavior.

Consequences

GENERATION GAP provides the following four benefits:

1. *Modifications are decoupled from generated code.* All hand-modifications go into ExtensionClass, encapsulating them and keeping them separate from generated code. As a bonus, the ExtensionClass interface may offer insight into the modification by indicating the operations that were overridden or added.
2. *Modifications can have privileged access to implementation details.* The inheritance relationship between CoreClass and ExtensionClass means that programmers and tool builders can leverage the full expressiveness of the implementation language to control access to generated internals.

3. *Subsequent regeneration does not require reapplying the modifications.* The tool regenerates only CoreClass, not ExtensionClass, thereby preserving the modifications across generations. Even though the modifications will not need to be reapplied, they may need modification themselves if either of the following is true:

    - The modifications refer to members that no longer exist (an example of "syntactic incompatibility").

    - The regenerated code differs semantically from its previous incarnation so that operations no longer mean the same thing ("semantic incompatibility").

    Syntactic incompatibility is usually easier to correct than semantic incompatibility. Both incompatibilities diminish the pattern's effectiveness, so they must not be inherent to the code being generated.

4. *CoreClass and ExtensionClass may be developed and tested independently.* The larger a software development project is, the more likely it'll involve people with specialized skills. Those with domain expertise might focus on modeling or analysis while others specialize in design, implementation, testing, or documentation. The challenge here is to ensure that these groups collaborate efficiently and that their outputs integrate smoothly. The more independent groups are, the more they can accomplish in parallel, but the harder the integration phase tends to be.

    GENERATION GAP promotes conflict-free collaboration and integration by decoupling CoreClass and ExtensionClass functionality. Regarding the Motivation example, a user interface specialist can develop Clock_core with the builder while a domain expert integrates Clock into the underlying application framework. Once developers have settled on a Clock_core interface, they can work independently.

    The pattern also lets developers test core and extension classes separately. Before modification, Clock_core is instantiable and has some utility. The user interface specialist can use the builder's output to evaluate the appearance, ergonomics, performance, and other aspects of the user interface that Clock isn't likely to affect. Meanwhile the domain expert can test the subsystems that underlie the user interface by modifying Clock and exercising it programmatically—that is, without assembling or even instantiating widgets. Once the parties are satisfied with their respective classes, integrating them should be easy.

There are two main liabilities of the pattern:

1. *Double the number of classes.* The pattern introduces a Core-Class/ExtensionClass pair for every class that would have been used. It may also introduce classes where there had been none, if for example the generated code was essentially procedural. Each class in a system costs you something, if not storage or execution speed, then at least conceptual overhead.

2. *Integrating generated classes into existing class hierarchies may be difficult.* Making the *extension class* inherit from an existing class requires multiple inheritance. You could achieve the same effect by having CoreClass inherit from the existing class, but that involves changing the CoreClass interface, defeating the purpose of the pattern. This problem can be addressed in the code generator by letting the user specify a parent class for the core class.

Implementation

GENERATION GAP's implementation depends a lot on both the programming environment and the programming language. Consider the following four issues:

1. *Disallowing modifications to the core class.* GENERATION GAP's cardinal requirement is that programmers never modify the core class. Unfortunately, ensuring that can be a challenge.

    In a file-based programming language and environment, the most secure way to preclude such changes is to place the class declaration and implementation in one or more write-protected files. However, the files cannot be so well protected that the tool can't overwrite them when it regenerates the code. You might need to give the tool special privileges independent of its user's privileges.

Things might be easier in a programming environment that uses some sort of database to store program information. These environments usually offer finer-grained access control to program source than can be had with conventional file systems.

2. *Controlling access to core class internals.* As we saw in the Motivation section, the extension class might need to access internal core class functionality. The inheritance relationship between the core and extension classes makes that easy, because in most object-oriented languages, a subclass can access potentially everything it inherits from its parent class.

   Keep in mind, though, that the more information CoreClass exposes to subclasses, the more likely regenerating the code will break modifications to ExtensionClass. Languages such as C++, Java, and Eiffel offer several levels of access control for hiding information from subclasses. By controlling access to core class internals, the code generator can minimize the assumptions an extension class makes about its core class.

3. *Naming conventions.* Because the pattern often splits one class into two, the names of the resulting core and extension classes should reflect their origin and close relationship. Nevertheless, the split is immaterial to clients. Therefore ExtensionClass should retain the name of the original class, and CoreClass should derive its name from its subclass—the opposite of normal. In the builder example, "_core" was appended to the name of the extension class to produce the core class name.

4. *Granularity of CoreClass operations.* The main benefit of code generation is that it raises the level at which one programs. Often the code generator must produce lots of code to implement a high-level metaphor. As a result, the programmer who wants to modify or extend the generated code will be oblivious to most of its intricacies. How then can we expect him or her to change it?

   The key to this problem lies in the CoreClass interface. The operations must be fine-grained enough so that programmers can override precisely the functionality they're interested in and reuse the rest. If, for example, CoreClass implemented everything in one big operation, then a programmer couldn't make even small changes in functionality without reimplementing the whole operation. If on the other hand, CoreClass breaks up that operation into a template method comprising several small and judiciously chosen primitive operations (such as factory methods), then it's more likely the programmer can modify or extend just the functionality he or she wants.

Sample Code

Here is the actual declaration of the Clock_core class as generated by the *ibuild* graphical user interface (GUI) builder [VT91]:

```
class Clock_core : public MonoScene {
public:
    Clock_core(const char*);
protected:
    Interactor* Interior();

    virtual void setTime();
    virtual void setAlarm();
    virtual void snooze();
protected:
    Picture* _clock;
    SF_Polygon* _hour_hand;
    SF_Rect* _min_hand;
    Line* _sec_hand;
};
```

MonoScene is a Decorator class for widgets in the InterViews GUI toolkit [LVC89]. Interactor is the base class for widgets in Inter-Views; thus MonoScene is an Interactor. InterViews also furnishes the SF_Polygon, SF_Rect, Line, and Picture classes, which implement graphical objects. Picture is a Composite class from the COMPOSITE pattern, while the other classes act as Leaf classes in that pattern. *ibuild*'s user exported these instances to make them accessible to the extension class.

Although Clock_core appears to define just a few member functions, its interface is really quite large, mainly because Interactor's interface is. Clock_core inherits a lot of default behavior too, both from Interactor and from MonoScene. Of the operations Clock_core adds, only Interior actually does anything: It assembles the widgets and graphical objects (both exported and nonexported ones) to form the user interface. Interior is nonvirtual because the assembly is specified entirely in the builder, so there's never a need to override it—you'd just redraw the user interface in the builder.

But we do need to add some behavior programmatically. To add behavior, we modify the extension class. Here's what it looks like before modification:

```
class Clock : public Clock_core {
public:
    Clock(const char*);
};
```

The constructor does nothing. Yet thanks to all the generated code Clock inherits, it is a fully instantiable class that displays a clock face, albeit with no behavior. We just need to override some operations.

setTime, setAlarm, and snooze were specified in the builder. They are the operations that the corresponding buttons invoke when they're pressed. They do nothing by default; we override them in Clock to do useful work. We also need to add code for rotating the hands in response to InterViews timer events, which the clock needs to receive every second.

The modifications to make this class a full-fledged application are straightforward:

```
class Clock : public Clock_core {
public:
    Clock(const char*);

    void run();

    virtual void setTime();
    virtual void setAlarm();
    virtual void snooze();

    virtual void Update();

private:
    void getSystemTime(int& h, int& m, int& s);
    void setSystemTime(int h, int m, int s);
    void alarm();

private:
    float _time;
    float _alarm;
};
```

The modified constructor initializes _alarm, which stores the alarm time, and _time, the time of the last update, to zero. run implements the event loop. It waits up to 1 second for input events and then updates the clock's appearance to reflect the current time as reported by getSystemTime.

run is a template method that has alarm and Update as primitive operations. It calls alarm when the alarm should go off, and it calls Update (inherited from Interactor, by the way) to update the clock's appearance. To minimize redrawing, Update determines the amount of rotation for each hand from the difference between the current and last update times. That way it rotates only what has to move.

setTime, setAlarm, and snooze are overridden to do their jobs. In particular, setTime and setAlarm must pop up dialog boxes—created with *ibuild*, of course—to collect data from the user. getSystemTime and setSystemTime are just helper functions that encapsulate system calls for getting and setting the system time.

Known Uses

ibuild [VT91] pioneered the use of GENERATION GAP in a user interface builder.

That's where I stopped in the original article, adding rather sheepishly that lack of other known uses was what deep-sixed the pattern's inclusion in *Design Patterns*. I also took the opportunity to solicit examples from my readers, and the responses were many. David Van Camp [VanCamp96] wrote,

> [A]s I read your pattern, I suddenly recalled a tool which shipped with Symantec C++ 6.0 for Windows/DOS called Visual Programmer, from Blue Sky Software. I've always been impressed with Blue Sky's tools, and this was no exception. As I recall, Visual Programmer automatically generated two sets of source files—one was the generated code and the second was a set of empty classes for modification as desired by the user (e.g., GENERATION GAP). Copyright on the manual is 1993, so this was a while ago. I never really used the tool, but I remember that it impressed me greatly.

David also gave a reference to Forté Express, an application builder for distributed environments [Forté97]. Express uses a variation of GENER-ATION GAP to let you slip custom code between Forté's library code and the code Express generates.

In case you're thinking this pattern is only good for builders, Chris Clark and Barbara Zino [CZ96] offer a counterexample:

> We use a variation on [GENERATION GAP] in Yacc++ and the Language Objects Library. As might be expected from the name, our tool generates lexers and parsers from language descriptions. More important, the tool comes with a library which embodies the framework of a typical compiler front-end. The actual transition tables are generated by the tool and need to be mated to the appropriate [lexing and parsing] engine *[an example of STRATEGY—J.V.]*. Therefore, the tool generates a class derived from the appropriate engine class when generating the user-specified class. This separation is similar to the GENERATION GAP split you mentioned. The implementation code and instance variables are in the library class. The derived class is free to override any of the member functions that need to be customized.

Several people suggested CORBA stub generation as an example. Gerolf Wendland was particularly thorough in this regard [Wendland97], going so far as to include great swaths of code (which I've omitted) from Jon Siegel's *CORBA Fundamentals and Programming* [Siegel96]. Gerolf wrote,

> The Orbix CORBA implementation applies a similar pattern (perhaps exactly the same). I'll send you example code that is taken from the book.
>
> [A]ssume that the (CORBA-compliant) BOA approach is employed. Let's take as an example the interface StoreAccess. This is compiled by the IDL compiler which in turn generates the class StoreAccessBOA-Impl. This class contains all functionality that is necessary to cooperate with the Orbix run-time system and, of course, the operations that were previously specified in the IDL description.
>
> To provide your own operations, you have to subclass StoreAccess-BOAImpl and override the operations from the IDL description. The programmer is free in naming the subclass; Orbix suggests the convention StoreAccess_i ([for] implementation).
>
> The Orbix IDL compiler provides a means to have code skeletons for StoreAccess_i generated. However, once you have used, and extended, these skeletons, you cannot have the skeletons regenerated without loss of all changes. But it is possible to have the files that contain [the] defi-

nition and implementation of class StoreAccessBOAImpl regenerated as often as you like.

Your naming scheme would map to Orbix's naming scheme this way:

StoreAccessBOAImpl ⇔ StoreAccess_core

StoreAccessBOAImpl_i (e.g.) ⇔ StoreAccess

Interesting. Judging from this and all the other feedback, I think it's safe now to certify GENERATION GAP as having a critical mass of known uses.

There's just one more section to recount before we're done.

Related Patterns

Core classes often use template methods to make generated code flexible and reusable. Factory methods can give extension classes control over the objects that the core class uses internally, such as Strategies.

I've always held a special place in my heart for GENERATION GAP, even when it didn't make the cut as a bona fide pattern. It transformed *ibuild* from a tool that generated highly functional but hard-to-maintain code, suitable only for the first cut at a user interface, into a real application-building workhorse supporting not only the GUI but some behavior as well. We may not have known whether others had applied this pattern, but I certainly wasn't surprised to learn many had.

If you're into code generation of any object-oriented sort, give GENERATION GAP a try. And please let me know how you use it, especially if it's in a way I haven't described. That's the thing about known uses—it's hard to have too many.

Type Laundering

Something's wrong. Things are getting ugly.

You're jumping through hoops trying to recover lost type information. Over and over you find yourself using the D-word—dynamic_cast. But you've got no choice, because the silly framework you're using doesn't know about the extensions you've made to its interfaces. This sort of suffering is a sure sign of a design bug. The good news is that bugs have a way of turning into features, in this case a rather useful one.

Picture a real-time control framework that defines an abstract base class Event. An application based on this framework uses subclasses of Event to model domain-specific events. Different applications will need different kinds events: those generated by, say, a cruise missile will be rather different from those of a vending machine, unless it's designed for particularly tough neighborhoods.

Given the diversity of domain-specific events, the framework's designer didn't even try to come up with the be-all and end-all Event interface. Instead, Event defines just a couple of operations that make sense for any and all kinds of events:

```
virtual long timestamp() = 0;
virtual const char* rep() = 0;
```

timestamp defines the precise time of an event's occurrence, and rep returns a low-level representation of the event, perhaps a packet of bytes straight from the network or device under control. It's the job of subclasses to define and implement more specific and application-friendly operations.

Take the vending machine. Its CoinInsertedEvent subclass adds a Cents getCoin() operation that returns the value of the coin a customer deposited. Another kind of event, CoinReleaseEvent, gets instantiated when the customer wants his or her money back. getCoin and similar operations would be implemented using rep. Clients of these events could, of course, use rep directly, if it's public. But there's little reason to make it so: rep offers almost no abstraction, and it makes clients work pretty hard to get at the information they need. More likely, rep would be protected—of interest only to subclasses, which use it to implement more specialized interfaces.

There's a problem lurking here, however, and it stems from the inability to define a universal interface for events. The framework doesn't and can't know anything about domain-specific Event subclasses. After all, they're defined by application programmers long after the framework was designed, developed, and stamped onto CD-ROM. All the framework knows about events is that they implement a bare-bones interface comprising `timestamp` and `rep` operations.

That begs two questions:

1. How does the framework *create instances* of domain-specific subclasses?

2. How does application code *access subclass-specific operations* when all it gets from the framework is objects of type Event?

An answer to the first question lies in any one of several creational patterns described in *Design Patterns*. For example, the framework can define factory methods (from the FACTORY METHOD pattern) that return instances of domain-specific Event subclasses. Whenever the framework needs a new instance, it uses a factory method instead of calling `new`. An application overrides these factory methods to return domain-specific instances.

If you don't want to have to subclass just to return domain-specific events, then use the PROTOTYPE pattern. PROTOTYPE offers a compositional alternative to FACTORY METHOD. By adding a

```
virtual Event* copy()
```

operation to the Event base class, framework code can use events to create copies of themselves. So instead of writing

```
Event* e = new CoinReleaseEvent;
```

which the framework can't possibly do because it refers to a domain-specific subclass, we write

```
Event* e = prototype->copy();
```

where `prototype` points to an instance of a type known to the framework, namely Event. Because `copy` is a polymorphic operation, e can be an instance of *any* Event subclass, domain-specific or not. The framework implementor just has to make sure `prototype` gets initialized before it's used, specifically to an instance of the proper Event subclass. That's something that an application can do in its initialization phase or at any convenient time before the framework calls `prototype->copy()`.

So much for creating subclass-specific instances. Now for the second question: Are there patterns for recovering type information from an instance? More precisely, if the framework provides an operation like

```
virtual Event* nextEvent();
```

how does an application know which kind of event nextEvent returns so that it can call the right subclass-specific operations?

Well, there's always the brute-force approach:

```
Event* e = nextEvent();
CoinInsertedEvent* ie;
CoinReleaseEvent* re;
// similar declarations for other kinds of events

if (ie = dynamic_cast<CoinInsertedEvent*>(e)) {
    // call CoinInsertedEvent-specific operations on ie

} else if (re = dynamic_cast<CoinReleaseEvent*>(e)) {
    // call CoinReleaseEvent-specific operations on re

} else if (...) {
    // ...you get the idea
}
```

It would be painful indeed to have to do this everywhere the application handles an event from the framework. And that's not the end of it: The pain intensifies later if and when we define a new subclass of Event. There's got to be a better way.

VISITOR is our standard technique for recovering lost type information without resorting to dynamic casts. The first step in applying the pattern here is to add a void accept(EventVisitor&) operation to the Event base class, where EventVisitor is the base class for objects that can visit events. Since the framework defines the Event class, it must also define the EventVisitor class—at which point we hit another roadblock: What does EventVisitor's interface look like?

We know the abstract Visitor interface must define visit operations for each kind of object a visitor can visit. But what if the types of these objects are unknown to the framework? Our visitor of vending machine events would need operations like these:

```
virtual void visit(CoinInsertedEvent*);
virtual void visit(CoinReleaseEvent*);
// and so forth, a visit operation for each
// domain-specific event
```

Obviously, these operations can't be defined by a framework class like EventVisitor. Looks like even VISITOR can't save us from the dreaded `dynamic_cast`. Sigh.

Despite appearances, the point here is not to bemoan the loss of type information but to use it to our advantage. Forget about Event for now and consider a seemingly unrelated issue in the MEMENTO pattern. (Not to worry—I'll examine a radically different solution to Event's travails a little later.)

MEMENTO's intent is to capture and externalize an object's state so that the object can be restored to that state sometime later. That may sound easy, but I've left out an important constraint: Externalizing the state must be done *without violating the object's encapsulation.* In other words, the object's internal state should be *available* but not *visible* to other objects. Contradictory, no?

Nope. A simple example will illustrate the distinction. As we describe in ITERATOR, a *cursor* is an iterator that does nothing but mark a position in a traversal. During traversal, the structure being traversed "advances" the cursor, which makes it point to the next element in the traversal. The structure can also "dereference" the cursor (that is, return the element it points to) on a client's behalf, like so:

```
Structure s;
Cursor c;

for (s.first(c); s.more(c); s.next(c)) {
    Element e = s.element(c);
    // use Element e
}
```

The cursor has no client-accessible operations. Only the structure being traversed can access the cursor's internals. The structure deserves exclusive privilege because the information in the cursor is actually part of the structure's internal state. As such it must remain encapsulated—and that's why the cursor is a Memento. As for the other participants in the pattern, the structure is the memento's Originator, and the client acts as Caretaker.

The key to pulling this off is to implement what amounts to a two-faced object. The structure sees a wide interface that allows access to state information. Other clients see a narrow or even nonexistent Memento interface; to give them access to any state inside the memento would be to compromise the structure's encapsulation. But how do we give an object two different interfaces in C++?

The MEMENTO pattern suggests using the friend keyword. The Originator is a friend of the Memento, permitting access to a wide interface while denying access to other classes.

```cpp
class Cursor {
public:
    virtual ~Cursor();

private:
    friend class Structure;

    Cursor () { _current = 0; }

    ListElem* getCurrent () const { return _current; }
    void setCurrent (ListElem* e) { _current = e; }

private:
    ListElem* _current;
};
```

In this scenario, Cursor keeps just a li'l ol' pointer. It points to a ListElem, a class that Structure uses internally to represent nodes in a doubly-linked list. ListElem objects maintain a pointer to the predecessor and successor in the list, along with a pointer to an Element object. Structure operations manipulate _current to keep track of the point in the traversal:

```cpp
class Structure {
public:
    // ...

    virtual void first (Cursor& c) {
        c.setCurrent(_head);
            // _head is the head of the linked list,
            // which Structure keeps internally
    }
```

```
        virtual bool more (const Cursor& c) {
            return c.getCurrent()->_next;
        }

        virtual void next (Cursor& c) {
            c.setCurrent(c.getCurrent()->_next);
                // set current to next ListElem*
        }

        virtual Element& element (const Cursor& c) {
            return *c.getCurrent()->_element;
        }
        // ...
    };
```

In sum, MEMENTO lets the structure furrow away just enough sensitive information in the `Cursor` Memento to mark the current stage of a traversal.

Connoisseurs of `friend` may notice a potentially serious shortcoming of this approach. Because friendship isn't inherited, a `Substructure` subclass of `Structure` doesn't have the access privileges of its parent. In other words, `Substructure` code can't access `Cursor`'s secret interface.

This is really no big deal if `Substructure` merely inherits its cursor-handling operations from `Structure`. But if `Substructure` needs to override these operations, or if it must implement other cursor-dependent functionality, it won't be able to use the private `Cursor` operations. For example, suppose `Substructure` keeps its own linked list of subelements that should be included in traversals. When `next` reaches the end of `Structure`'s linked list, it advances to the head of `Substructure`'s list transparently. That will require overriding `next` and setting the cursor's `_current` member appropriately.

One work-around would be to define protected operations in `Structure` that parallel `Cursor`'s interface, except they delegate their implementation to a cursor:

```
class Structure {
    // ...

protected:
    ListElem* getCurrent (const Cursor& c) const {
        return c.getCurrent();
    }
```

```
void setCurrent (Cursor& c, ListElem* e) {
    c.setCurrent(e);
}
// ...
};
```

That effectively extends Structure's privileges to its subclasses. But parallel interfaces are usually a mistake. They're ugly, they're redundant, and they make changing an interface that much more work. If we can avoid them—or better yet, avoid friend altogether—we'll probably end up thanking ourselves in the long run.

Here's where we turn a design bug into a feature. I even have a name for it: *type laundering*. The idea is to define Cursor as an abstract base class that includes only those aspects of its interface that should be public, which in this case is just the destructor:

```
class Cursor {
public:
    virtual ~Cursor () { }

protected:
    Cursor();
    Cursor(const Cursor&);
};
```

We protect the default and copy constructors to preclude instantiation—that is, to ensure Cursor acts as an abstract class. We could do the same thing merely by declaring the destructor pure virtual, but that forces subclasses to define the destructor even if they don't need to. Either way, subclasses define the privileged interface:

```
class ListCursor : public Cursor {
public:
    ListCursor () { _current = 0; }

    ListElem* getCurrent () const { return _current; }
    void setCurrent (ListElem* e) { _current = e; }

private:
    ListElem* _current;
};
```

In this arrangement, Structure operations that take a Cursor as an argument must downcast it to a ListCursor before they can access the extended interface:

```
class Structure {
public:
    // ...

    virtual void first (Cursor& c) {
        ListCursor* lc;

        if (lc = dynamic_cast<ListCursor*>(&c)) {
            lc->setCurrent(_head);
                // _head is the head of the linked list,
                // which Structure keeps internally
        }
    }
    // ...
};
```

The dynamic cast ensures that the structure will access and modify ListCursor objects and only ListCursor objects.

The final flourish to this design is how cursors get instantiated. Obviously, clients can no longer instantiate Cursor or its subclasses directly—only a Structure (subclass) knows the kind of cursor it uses. Instead we use a variation on FACTORY METHOD to abstract the instantiation process:

```
class Structure {
public:
    // ...

    virtual Cursor* cursor () { return new ListCursor; }
    // ...
};
```

Because cursor() returns something of type Cursor*, clients can't access the subclass-specific operations unless they start (dynamic) casting randomly to figure out the type—and even that's not an option if ListCursor isn't exported in a header file. Meanwhile, Structure subclasses are free to redefine cursor-manipulating operations such as more, next, and element.

Figure 3.11 summarizes the type laundering-based implementation. Compare it to MEMENTO's Structure diagram on page 285 of *Design Patterns*. The main difference here is the introduction of a Concrete-Memento subclass, which adds the privileged interface to the bare-bones Memento interface. Originators know they're dealing with con-

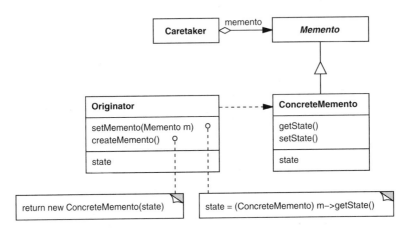

FIGURE 3.11 *Revised Structure diagram for type-laundering* MEMENTO

crete mementos (they instantiate them, after all). But caretakers can do next to nothing with mementos, because all they see are the bare bones. Although this diagram can't show it, type laundering absolves a C++ implementation from using `friend` and having to work around its shortcomings.

Amazing how a little type laundering can clean up your design. (Cough!)

Thanks for the Memory Leaks

Okay, so I lied when I described the implementation of `cursor()` as the "final flourish" to this design. If we were implementing this approach in a garbage-collected language, I would have been telling the truth. But in the context of C++, I've made the client responsible for deleting the cursor that `cursor()` creates—allowing ample opportunity for memory leaks. Returning a `Cursor*` rather than a `Cursor&` also makes for unsightly dereferences when we pass the heap-allocated cursor to operations like `first` and `more`.

We can get around both problems by applying Dijkstra's panacea: adding a level of indirection. Specifically, we'll implement a variant of Cope's Handle-Body idiom [Coplien92]. Instead of having `Cursor` as our abstract Memento base class, we'll define a "body" class, Cursor-Imp, to act in its place:

```
class CursorImp {
public:
    virtual ~CursorImp () { }

    void ref ()   { ++_count; }
    void unref () { if (--_count == 0) delete this; }
protected:
    CursorImp ()   { _count = 0; }
    CursorImp (const Cursor&);

private:
    int _count;
};
```

Like most "bodies" in the Handle-Body idiom, CursorImp objects are reference-counted. Concrete subclasses of CursorImp are Concrete-Mementos; that is, they define privileged interfaces. Thus our List-Cursor example becomes

```
class ListCursorImp : public CursorImp {
public:
    ListCursorImp () { _current = 0; }

    ListElem* getCurrent () const { return _current; }
    void setCurrent (ListElem* e) { _current = e; }
        // same privileged operations as before

private:
    ListElem* _current;
};
```

Now comes the key difference between this approach and the original: Clients don't deal with CursorImp objects directly. Instead, we introduce a concrete Cursor class to act as a "handle" to our CursorImp body:

```
class Cursor {
public:
    Cursor (CursorImp* i) { _imp = i; _imp->ref(); }

    Cursor (Cursor& c) {
        _imp = c.imp();
        _imp->ref();
    }
```

```
    ~Cursor ()              { _imp->unref(); }

    CursorImp* imp ()       { return _imp; }
private:
    static void* operator new (size_t)  { return 0; }
    static void operator delete (void *) { }

    Cursor& operator = (Cursor& c)      { return c; }
        // disallow heap allocation and assignment for
        // simplicity and to avert common mishaps
private:
    CursorImp* _imp;
};
```

As a handle, `Cursor` aggregates an instance of a `CursorImp` subclass.
`Cursor` also sees to it that the instance is reference-counted correctly.
An originator employs these classes to return what appears to be a
purely stack-allocated `Cursor` object:

```
class Structure {
public:
    // ...

    virtual Cursor cursor () {
        return Cursor(new ListCursorImp);
    }
    // ...
};
```

`cursor()` returns a `Cursor`, not a reference to one, thereby ensuring
that clients will invoke the copy constructor:

```
Structure s;
Cursor c = s.cursor(); // sole modification to original
                       // example on page 105

for (s.first(c); s.more(c); s.next(c)) {
    Element e = s.element(c);
    // use Element e
}
```

Note that there's no need to dereference c, as is the case with the original, pointer-returning version of `cursor()`.

The only other change we need to make is in the code that does the
dynamic cast to recover the ConcreteMemento:

```
class Structure {
    // ...

    virtual void first (Cursor& c) {
        ListCursorImp* imp;

        if (imp = dynamic_cast<ListCursorImp*>(c.imp())) {
            imp->setCurrent(_head);
        }
    }

    // ...
};
```

Sure, this is a bit more complicated for the Memento implementor than the non-reference-counted version. But it makes the type laundering-based version as easy for clients to use as the `friend`-based version—which had some implementation intricacies of its own.

Still, I've never been wild about taking out the garbage. ;-)

Michael McCosker writes [McCosker97],

[Y]ou mention using a pure virtual destructor to force subclasses to define their own destructor. My understanding of C++ is that *all* destructors are called. In the environment I work in (Win32 on PCs), calling a destructor at address zero causes a page fault. Is this just a problem in this environment or should one never have a pure virtual destructor?

My preferred way to make a class abstract in C++ is by protecting constructors as opposed to making at least one member function pure virtual. The type-laundering example is, in part, an attempt to demonstrate the virtues of my preference. Here again is the class in question:

```
class Cursor {
public:
    virtual ~Cursor () { }

protected:
    Cursor();
    Cursor(const Cursor&);
};
```

The only other way to make Cursor abstract is by making the destructor pure virtual. But what the heck does a "pure virtual destructor" *mean?* Destructors aren't inherited per se; all of them get called sequentially. Therefore a pure virtual destructor must be defined. Is that possible?

You bet. Consider the following passage from the C++ draft standard [ASC96]:

> §10.4, paragraph 2: A pure virtual function need be defined only if explicitly called with the *qualified_id* syntax. . . . Note: a function declaration cannot provide both a *pure_specifier* and a definition.

Because the pure virtual destructor will in fact be called explicitly during destruction, this section indicates that it *must* be defined—not in the declaration, but in a separate definition:

```
class Cursor {
public:
    virtual ~Cursor () = 0;
};

Cursor::~Cursor () { }
```

I suppose there isn't a whole lot of difference between the two approaches after all. In one, you have to protect every constructor; in the other, you have to define a pure virtual destructor. It's *always something.*

Pushme-Pullyu

There's a problem I left unresolved in the real-time control example, and it concerns how the framework supplies events to application code. In the standard approach, the framework defines a

```
virtual Event* nextEvent();
```

operation that the application calls whenever and wherever it wants to handle an event. The unhappy consequence is that the return value must invariably be downcast to an application-defined type. In the vending machine case, that precipitated the following code:

```
Event* e = nextEvent();
CoinInsertedEvent* ie;
CoinReleaseEvent* re;
// similar declarations for other kinds of events

if (ie = dynamic_cast<CoinInsertedEvent*>(e)) {
    // call CoinInsertedEvent-specific operations on ie

} else if (re = dynamic_cast<CoinReleaseEvent*>(e)) {
    // call CoinReleaseEvent-specific operations on re

} else if (...) {
    // ...you get the idea
}
```

The framework knows only about the base class, Event. So whenever the framework deals with an event, it effectively "launders out" all type information beyond what Event declares—including all vestiges of subclass-defined extensions. Type information gets lost as a result, and we have to work hard to recover it.

In situations where interface extensions are the norm, this is no small annoyance. The event-handling code is not type-safe. The results of dynamic casts cannot be checked at compile-time, leaving discovery of type-related programming errors to crash-time. And then there are the classic drawbacks of tag-and-switch-style programming: The code is clumsy, it's hard to extend, and it's inefficient.

After an application of VISITOR failed to remedy the situation, I promised to describe a radically different approach. Here's the beef.

Part of what makes the new approach different is how events get delivered. Currently, nextEvent is *the* way an application gets events. Application code calls this operation when it's good and ready to process the next event. If it happens to call nextEvent when no event is pending, one of two things will occur: The calling thread will block, or nextEvent will return a null value, probably resulting in a busy–wait. It's up to the framework designer to decide which will be the case.[8] Either way, the consumer of the event initiates its handling. This is the **pull** model of event-driven programming, because the event con-

---

8. Many frameworks provide blocking *and* nonblocking analogs of next-Event in support of both options. Some also allow blocking with a timeout.

sumer (e.g., the application) is the active entity, "pulling" information from the event producer—the framework in this case.

The *yin* to this pull model *yang* is called, not surprisingly, the **push** model. There, the consumer passively awaits notification of an event's arrival. Because the producer must push information to arbitrarily many consumers, the model requires a priori registration of consumers with the producer(s) who should notify them.[9]

As far as we're concerned, the question of push versus pull boils down to establishing the locus of control in this framework. The push model tends to simplify the consumer at the producer's expense, while the pull model does the reverse. Ergo it's important to consider the relative abundance of producer and consumer code. If you have few producers and lots of consumers, then the push model is arguably the better option. In a circuit simulation, for example, there may be one global clock and many subcircuits that depend on it. So it's probably better to have a push-model clock, with its attendant complexity, than to complicate every subcircuit.

This isn't a hard-and-fast rule, mind you; there may be considerations that favor the pull model independent of the number of producing or consuming code sites. But in our real-time control framework, it's reasonable to assume there will be more loci of code for consuming events than for producing them. With counterarguments lacking, push becomes the model of choice.

The other key difference in this approach concerns centralization of the source of events—or rather the avoidance thereof. Currently, next-Event centralizes the event delivery mechanism in the framework, making it the type-laundering bottleneck that it is. So if centralization is the problem, isn't some form of *de*centralization the obvious solution?

No doubt, but first things first. If an extensible and type-safe event delivery mechanism is our ideal (and it is), then we should be careful where we put the interface that delivers events to application code—or at least the interface for delivering *application-specific* events. It cannot reside in the framework at all, lest we end up in dynamic_cast purga-

---

9. The push model is another example of "The Hollywood Principle" (page 45). For an in-depth treatment of both models, see the excellent article by Schmidt and Vinoski [SV97].

tory as before. We have to deliver events in a type-safe way *and* let applications define new kinds of events without changing code, be it code in the framework or the application. These constraints, together with the switch from pull to push, call for the demise of `nextEvent` as the sole interface for delivering events.

Now we have to figure out where to transfer that responsibility. Because extensibility is a concern, sooner or later we must consider what will change when one extends the system. Let's do it sooner and assume the change that concerns applications most in this context is the *definition of new events*. The framework, of course, may predefine some general-purpose events, like maybe TimerEvent or ErrorEvent. But most applications will define their own events on a higher level of abstraction—the vending machine's CoinInsertedEvent and Coin-ReleaseEvent classes, for example.

The granule of change, therefore, is the kind of event. I say that because matching the granule of *change* to the granule of *extension* is key to minimizing upheaval in the face of extension. A given change in functionality should call for a commensurate change in implementation. You clearly don't want a small functional change to provoke massive code modifications. But what about the converse? Why shouldn't a major change in functionality require only small changes to code?

That may seem desirable, but in fact it's utopian. Achieving it usually means one of two things: Either the system is functionally unstable and hence bug-prone, or, more likely, changes are expressed not in the system per se but in another, usually interpreted specification—a scripting language versus C++, for example. In the latter case, the system is unlikely to need modification only because "the system" refers to the interpreter. And rightly so: If adding functionality means changing the interpreter, then someone somewhere has failed spectacularly.

If you accept this matching principle as valid, then what are its implications for our design? We model each granule of change—the kind of event—explicitly as a class. A class defines both an implementation and an interface. By the matching principle, therefore, the code for extended functionality should comprise both implementation code *and* any specialized interfaces that clients need for type-safe access. In other words, a new kind of event should give rise to *one* new class, period. No other code should be added or changed.

To recap—the new design should (1) deliver events by pushing them to their consumers, and (2) require at most one new class per application-specific event, with no changes to existing code. Tall order, I know, but we'll very nearly achieve it.

First, forget about a common base class for events. Subclass-specific interfaces are the norm. There's hardly any base class functionality. There's no longer a nextEvent operation requiring a polymorphic return value. In sum, a common base class is more trouble than it's worth. So instead we define free-standing event classes having interfaces that are exactly what their clients need—no more, no less.

CoinInsertedEvent
Cents getCoin()

CoinReleaseEvent
CoinIterator coins()

ProductDispensedEvent
Product getProduct()

• • •

Next, each of these classes gets a unique registration interface:

CoinInsertedEvent
Cents getCoin() static register(CoinInsertedHandler) static notify(CoinInsertedEvent)

CoinReleaseEvent
CoinIterator coins() static register(CoinReleaseHandler) static notify(CoinReleaseEvent)

ProductDispensedEvent
Product getProduct() static register(ProductDispensedHandler) static notify(ProductDispensedEvent)

• • •

There are two registration-related operations: register and notify. Both are static. Any instance that's interested in getting CoinInserted-Events, for example, must register itself with the CoinInsertedEvent class. Any object can herald the arrival of a new CoinInsertedEvent instance by calling CoinInsertedEvent::notify with that instance as a parameter.

You may have noticed that you can't register just any old object with an event class; it has to be of a specific type. If you're confused, look at the argument of each register operation. For CoinInserted-Events the registrant must be of type CoinInsertedHandler, for Coin-ReleaseEvents it's CoinReleaseHandler, and so on. These types are defined in separate mixin classes that exist solely to define an event-handling interface:

CoinInsertedHandler
handle(CoinInsertedEvent)

CoinReleaseHandler
handle(CoinReleaseEvent)

ProductDispensedHandler
handle(ProductDispensedEvent)

• • •

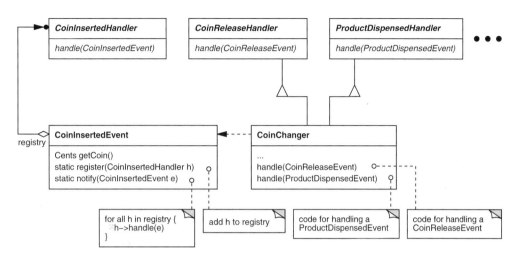

FIGURE 3.12 *CoinChanger implements both CoinReleaseHandler and ProductDispensedHandler interfaces*

A class that's interested in handling one or more of these events must implement the corresponding interfaces. For example, say a Coin-Changer class controls the behavior of the coin changer subsystem in the vending machine. The coin changer wants to know when the user presses the coin release button so that it can dispense change, if need be. It also wants to know when a product gets dispensed successfully so that it can reset itself for the next consignment. CoinChanger must therefore implement *both* the CoinReleaseHandler and Product-DispensedHandler interfaces, as Figure 3.12 shows.

Finally, the coin changer is responsible for notifying other subsystems about coin insertions. When the underlying hardware senses a coin, CoinChanger responds by creating a CoinInsertedEvent instance (as the dashed line with an arrowhead in Figure 3.12 suggests). After initializing the event with requisite information, it calls `CoinInserted-Event::notify`, passing the new instance as a parameter.

In turn, `notify` iterates through all the registered implementors of the CoinInsertedHandler interface—that is, all objects that have expressed interest in coin insertions—calling their `handle` operation and passing along the CoinInsertedEvent object. Meanwhile, the Coin-Changer object is registered, probably during instantiation, with the

CoinReleaseEvent and ProductDispensedEvent classes. Thus, whenever other subsystems in the vending machine produce CoinReleaseEvents or ProductDispensedEvents, the CoinChanger instance will find out about it. No type tests, no downcasting, no switch statements—no kidding.

Extension is easy too. Say a new model of vending machine comes with a bill changer, which calls for integrating a new BillAcceptedEvent into the control software. All that entails is defining a BillAcceptedEvent class plus a corresponding BillAcceptedHandler mixin. Then, any subsystem that cares about the new event has to do three things:

1. Register with BillAcceptedEvent

2. Inherit from BillAcceptedHandler

3. Implement `BillAcceptedHandler::handle` to handle the event

Yes, that's a bit short of the goal of defining only one new class and changing no existing code. We are introducing an extra interface (BillAcceptedHandler), but that doesn't amount to much work. And the changes to existing code are limited to the application, not the framework, which can content itself with a fixed set of predefined event classes and handler interfaces. Life *has* gotten better.

Mark Betz writes [Betz97],

[Y]ou resolve the "type-laundering" issue as it applies to handling of events in the control framework. Decentralization is one solution, but it has an effect that I didn't see directly acknowledged: Haven't you decentralized event handling until it was driven right out of the framework?

Yes and no. The framework can still define event classes and handlers for common events. I mentioned two, TimerEvent and ErrorEvent. Decentralization doesn't preclude reuse; the two are independent.

If event handling is to be type-safe, which was the point of the exercise, then the framework must avoid binding a particular type of event to the handling of that event. That's the goal of decentralization. When the framework defines the lone event-handling interface by binding event to handler, it must assume a lowest-common-denominator event type. Applications must make up the difference dynamically.

That may be a reasonable trade-off, by the way. Static typing is more of a hindrance than a help in many circumstances—after all, 50,000 Smalltalkers can't be wrong! But the larger and longer-lived the system, the more likely it is to benefit from static typing.

By the way, what you've witnessed here is an application of MULTI-CAST, a pattern we've done a lot of tinkering with. I'll take a closer look at it next.

CHAPTER 4

Labor of Love

MULTICAST was always a pattern in progress, assuming it was ever a pattern at all. Still, I thought it might be amusing to present it here in all its half-baked and disheveled glory. I've even included many of our exchanges on it, which should be even more amusing. Maybe *too* amusing. After all, people will realize we're no more prescient than anyone else. Those who ascribe extraordinary powers to the Gang of Four will be appalled by our generally chaotic process of pattern development. I might burst a bubble or two—which would be a good thing, come to think of it.

I'll hold off on the pivotal Intent section, always a bone of contention, and skip to the Motivation. The scenario here is similar but not identical to the vending machine example I've been using.

Motivation

A program is **event-driven** if its flow of control is governed by external stimuli called **events**. Event-driven designs are common in real-time control applications. A key design challenge lies in making these systems extensible and type-safe at the same time.

Consider a modern, digitally controlled vending machine. It has several subsystems, including a snack dispenser, a coin changer, a

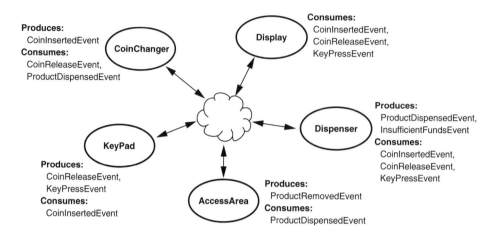

Produces:
  CoinInsertedEvent
Consumes:
  CoinReleaseEvent,
  ProductDispensedEvent

Consumes:
  CoinInsertedEvent,
  CoinReleaseEvent,
  KeyPressEvent

Produces:
  ProductDispensedEvent,
  InsufficientFundsEvent
Consumes:
  CoinInsertedEvent,
  CoinReleaseEvent,
  KeyPressEvent

Produces:
  CoinReleaseEvent,
  KeyPressEvent
Consumes:
  CoinInsertedEvent

Produces:
  ProductRemovedEvent
Consumes:
  ProductDispensedEvent

FIGURE 4.1 *Vending machine events, their producers, and their consumers*

keypad for selecting products, an alphanumeric display, and a "black box"—a simple computer that controls it all. The interactions between these subsystems and the customer get quite complicated. You can manage the complexity by modeling both the subsystems and the interactions among them as objects.

When a customer deposits a coin, for example, the CoinChanger object (which monitors the coin changer subsystem) produces a Coin-InsertedEvent object. This object records details of the event, including the time of the deposit and its amount in cents. Additional classes model other events of interest. A KeyPressEvent denotes the press of a key on the keypad. An instance of CoinReleaseEvent records a customer's request for his or her money back. ProductDispensedEvent and ProductRemovedEvent objects mark the final stages of a snack's consignment. The number of event classes may be large and potentially open-ended: Adding a bill changer and its associated events (e.g., BillInsertedEvent) should require minimal changes to existing code.

What happens after an event gets created? Which object(s) will use the event, and how does it get to them? The answers to these questions depend on the kind of event (see Figure 4.1). CoinChanger is interested in any CoinReleaseEvents that occur after a coin has been deposited. But a CoinChanger won't want to receive the CoinInsertedEvents it creates for other objects. Similarly, a Dispenser object generates in-

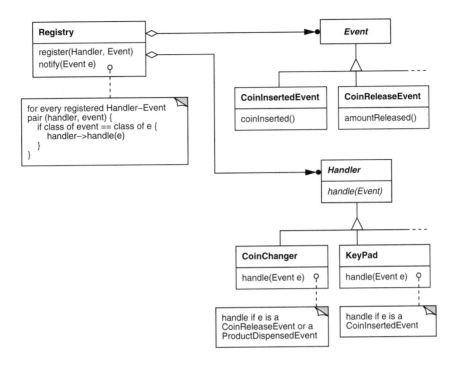

FIGURE 4.2 *Event registry approach*

stances of ProductDispensedEvent but isn't interested in receiving them. It will be keenly interested in KeyPressEvent objects, however, since they determine which snack to dispense. The interests of different subsystem objects vary, perhaps even dynamically.

What's developing here is a rat's nest of dependencies between event objects, their producers, and their consumers. Complex dependencies are undesirable because they make the system harder to understand, maintain, and modify. It should be easy to change an object's event interest not just statically but at run-time as well.

A common solution uses an **event registry** to keep track of these dependencies. Clients register interest in a particular event with the registry. After creating an event, an object passes it to the registry, which delivers it to the interested objects. This approach requires two standard interfaces—one for events and another for the objects that want to handle them (Figure 4.2).

When an instance of a Handler subclass, such as CoinChanger, receives an event through its `handle` operation (which implements CoinChanger's handling of the event), the event's concrete type is not known statically. That's significant because different kinds of events record different information; no single Event interface can anticipate the needs of every subclass. Therefore each Event subclass extends the basic Event interface with subclass-specific operations. To get at these operations, CoinChanger must attempt to downcast the event to a type it can handle:

```
void CoinChanger::handle (Event* e) {
    CoinReleaseEvent* cre;
    ProductDispensedEvent* pde;
    // similar declarations for other events of interest

    if (cre = dynamic_cast<CoinReleaseEvent*>(e)) {
        // handle a CoinReleaseEvent
    } else if (
        pde = dynamic_cast<ProductDispensedEvent*>(e)
    ) {
        // handle a ProductDispensedEvent
    } else if (...) {
        // etc.
    }
}
```

One problem with this approach is that it's not type-safe. Getting at the subclass-specific operations requires dynamic casts, the results of which cannot be checked at compile-time. This means that some type-related programming errors may remain hidden until run-time. This code has all the drawbacks of tag-and-switch-style programming as well: It's clumsy, it's hard to extend, and it's inefficient.

The MULTICAST pattern shows how to deliver information to interested objects in an extensible and statically type-safe manner. The pattern doesn't require singly rooted Event or Handler hierarchies. Instead, you define an abstract handler class for each concrete event class—for example, a CoinReleaseHandler for CoinReleaseEvent. Any class of objects that wants to handle CoinReleaseEvents must inherit from a CoinReleaseHandler class. The same goes for handling other types of events: Interested parties must inherit from the corresponding handler classes.

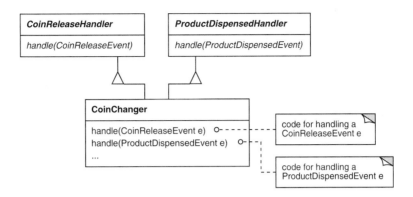

FIGURE 4.3 *Implementing Handler interfaces in CoinChanger*

In Figure 4.3, CoinChanger inherits from both CoinReleaseHandler and ProductDispensedHandler because it's interested in both Coin-ReleaseEvents and ProductDispensedEvents—it might have to dispense coins in either event. As before, each handler class defines a handle operation in which subclasses implement their handling of the event. But unlike the original registry approach, handle's argument provides the precise concrete type of event, so there's no need for downcasting—the operation is statically type-safe.

But how do events get *delivered* to interested objects—that is, who calls handle? You could define a Registry class with register and notify operations as before, except now there are numerous classes of handlers that aren't related by inheritance. Consequently, not one but several register operations are needed, one for each kind of handler. And you'll have to add a register operation to the Registry class whenever you define a new kind of event. In other words, you'll have to change existing code.

Decentralization provides a way around this difficulty. Instead of registering with one big registry, clients can register interest directly with the objects that create events. For example, if a client is interested in CoinInsertedEvents, it registers that interest with CoinChanger, the class that produces those events (see Figure 4.4).

Whenever CoinChanger generates a CoinInsertedEvent, it calls its notify operation to deliver the event to all registered CoinInserted-

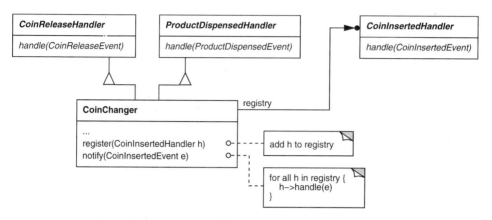

FIGURE 4.4 *CoinChanger registration interface and implementation*

Handlers. The compiler guarantees that the object they'll receive is precisely the kind they're interested in: CoinInsertedEvent.

Similarly, a client interested in ProductDispensedEvents registers itself with the Dispenser. In general, you register interest in a class of events with the instantiator(s) of that class. Decentralizing registration like this improves extensibility. When you define a new kind of event, the code you change is limited to the class(es) that create the events, whereas the centralized approach requires changing the registry's interface and implementation as well.

The main difference between the MULTICAST design and that of the preceding chapter is that, here, clients register event interest with the class that instantiates the event—CoinChanger in this case. The original design had clients registering with the event classes themselves. Actually, my first cut at the Motivation section did that too, but Erich objected:

> In my view, you register interest not with the event but with the *sender* of the event. In this case, the vending machine should have operations like addCoinReleaseHandler, addCoinInsertedHandler, etc.

I, on the other hand, feel it's important to motivate the case for putting the registration interface into the event classes. The impetus is ease of extension. You want to avoid upheaval when you define new kinds of events. If the registration mechanism is in an existing class, you'll have to change it to incorporate new registration operations. Putting the registration interface into the event itself makes it easier to accommodate new events.

From a modeling perspective, however, Erich is right, because notifying an event class may well seem unnatural. Even though we're talking about a static operation on a class and not an instance, it still looks as though you're notifying an event about itself!

Since Erich's preference constitutes a more general case, we agreed it should be the representative design. Hence the Structure, Participants, and Collaborations sections put the registration interface in the sender. Had I insisted on my preference, we'd end up confusing people by advocating a particular design in Motivation and a slightly different one thereafter.

❖ ❖ ❖

Structure

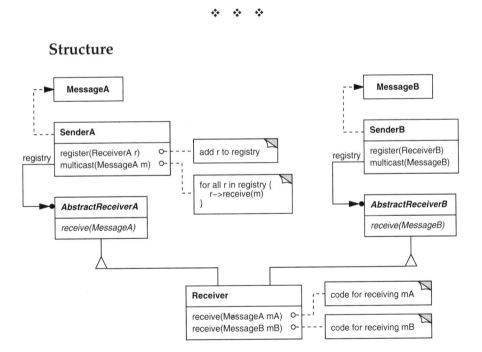

Participants

Message (ProductDispensedEvent)

- encapsulates information to be transferred from Sender to Receiver.

Sender (Dispenser)

- maintains a registry of Receiver objects.
- defines an interface for registering Receiver objects.
- defines and implements an interface for delivering a message to registered Receiver objects.

AbstractReceiver (ProductDispensedHandler)

- defines an interface for receiving a Message object.

Receiver (CoinChanger)

- implements one or more AbstractReceiver interfaces.

Collaborations

- Clients register receivers with senders through Sender's registration interface.
- Senders instantiate messages and deliver them to registered receivers.

The Structure, Participants, and Collaboration sections thus illustrate the general case. My earlier examples merely lump Sender and Message classes to form the Event classes. This remains a viable option, incidentally, so we relegated it to the Implementation section.

The four of us pretty much agree on the content so far, but seeds of dissension crop up in the Applicability section.

Applicability

Use MULTICAST when *all* of the following are true:

- Certain classes of objects may be interested in receiving information from other objects.
- The information is of arbitrary structure and complexity and may vary as the software evolves.
- The information transfer should be statically type-safe.

Although these points haven't elicited negative reactions by themselves, the last one may hold the crux of our differences. But let me explain our biases first. Erich, Richard, and I were weaned on C++, which is relatively strongly typed. Ralph is a Smalltalker—Smalltalk having no notion of static type checking. It's probably no coincidence then that while the rest of us think MULTICAST is worthy of design pattern status, Ralph thinks it's just a variation on the OBSERVER pattern. As such, he believes it should be written up as part of a new and expanded OBSERVER.

There are clear similarities between OBSERVER and MULTICAST as it's currently conceived. Both maintain dependencies between objects, both communicate information between the objects, and both emphasize extensibility, among other things. Yet most of us feel there's an essential difference. Erich expressed this sentiment early on:

> MULTICAST is very close to OBSERVER, but the distinction is subtle.

Subtle indeed. I wrestled with the distinction and came up with a strawman:

> In OBSERVER, you're talking about a one-to-many dependency. Before you apply the pattern, the subject and its observers would have likely been lumped into one object. OBSERVER partitions that object to give you flexibility, etc. OBSERVER worries little about the information that passes between them or the extensibility thereof—it focuses on notification and subject–observer consistency.
>
> MULTICAST focuses on the information that's passed between Sender and Receiver—its extensibility and type-safety. Moreover, the Sender and Receiver are usually unrelated in what they model, and the connections between them are much more unpredictable, and probably more dynamic too.

Ralph, bless his heart, was not convinced:

Once you implement OBSERVER, you will definitely get *very* interested in what passes back and forth! The pattern in the book doesn't talk enough about this. It gives hints about push versus pull and the like, but it is vague and uninformative. It needs to be much more concrete and discuss the problems that can arise when you use OBSERVER. In my opinion, the topics you discuss are all ones that anybody who uses OBSERVER for a large project will need to think about.

I don't believe [the bit about MULTICAST's Sender and Receiver being unrelated in what they model]. Maybe I am missing something. But in [the VisualWorks Smalltalk environment], senders and receivers tend to be unrelated, and connections can be very dynamic. Since VisualComponents (the typical Observer) and ValueModels (the typical Subject) are all extremely reusable and are usually mixed-and-matched, connections between them are pretty unpredictable as well.

Given the lack of any semblance of multiple interface inheritance in Smalltalk, it's no wonder Ralph thinks MULTICAST is little more than a wart on OBSERVER, or maybe a mutant OBSERVER. Do you suppose MULTICAST is more an idiom for strongly typed languages than a design pattern?

In a later message, Ralph posits why the rest of us believe MULTICAST is a worthy design pattern in its own right:

I think one of the unspoken reasons you think MULTICAST is important is because of static type checking. You are trying to avoid type casting. You have two different ways of avoiding it. One is to pass an Event that you can dispatch on. The other is to make separate Handler hierarchies. It seems to me that if you did the first, you would not need to do the second, so I am not sure why MULTICAST needs both. Maybe it is because you want to put the behavior in the Observer (i.e., the Handler), not the Event. But it is clear to me that OBSERVER needs to talk about how static type checking makes things complicated.

In summary, OBSERVER defines a rich space of design variations. I don't see any reason why MULTICAST is much different from the other variations. That is why OBSERVER is a *pattern* and not a reusable mechanism. It gets changed each time it is used. When you are talking about MULTICAST, you are really talking about some common and useful variations of OBSERVER. But you are packaging a particular set of variations, while other sets of variations are just as interesting and you are ignoring them. I believe it would be better to explore the entire space.

I have to agree with a lot of this, and judging from the silence, so did everyone else. But you can't keep dumping stuff into a pattern indefinitely. So rather than rebut these points, Erich asked a new and different question:

> Is it that bad to promote a significant refinement and variation of a pattern as a separate pattern? Instead of having 20 Implementation bullets, I prefer to have a separate pattern.

Herein lies an important issue we've been skirting, that of pattern scalability. Could it be the crux *within* the crux? I felt it might be:

> There's fertile new territory in making our patterns more scalable. For each of our patterns I've got a file for comments, feedback, and any new insights we've had. Many of these files have gotten pretty big. If we were to incorporate everything we've learned about, say SINGLETON, into the SINGLETON pattern, the result would be ungainly. Some of our patterns—OBSERVER and COMPOSITE come to mind—are arguably too long as it is.
>
> How do we promote "scalability"? Making each pattern into a pattern language is one possibility. But I confess to being underwhelmed by [much of what's been] written by that name. It would be a real win to come up with some kind of superstructure that encompasses the current patterns while making room for new insights, extensions, and variations. If there's one thing I'm learning from MULTICAST, it's that our patterns can't go on growing forever.

I also felt a need to come up for air and ask a few fundamental questions:

1. How are [MULTICAST and OBSERVER] related?
2. Are they dependent? If so, must we roll them into one pattern?
3. Is the one-to-many dependency of OBSERVER useful by itself?
4. Should every application of OBSERVER also be an application of MULTICAST?

Ralph's thought on question 1 is that MULTICAST is either a "special-case/extension" of OBSERVER, or it is a "composite" pattern that contains OBSERVER.[1] Both imply that the patterns are dependent, at least to a degree. His answers to the last two questions reinforce this impression:

---

1. "Composite" in this context refers to a combination of patterns, not the COMPOSITE pattern.

Is the one-to-many dependency of OBSERVER useful by itself? It is in simple systems. When life gets complicated, there are various ways to cope. Some of them are simpler than MULTICAST. For example, ValueModels eliminate a lot of case statements without making events be objects.

Should every application of OBSERVER also be an application of MULTI-CAST? I think the real question is, "If you are going to use MULTICAST, is it worthwhile using OBSERVER without MULTICAST?" I can see arguing "no," because the advantages of using a simpler mechanism in part of your system are probably overwhelmed by the complexity of having two mechanisms that do more or less the same thing, so designers will have to choose which one to use. Just use one, and they won't have to decide. Life will be easier.

If that is true, then maybe a GUI framework that is supposed to be scalable should use MULTICAST, since large applications will need it. This would be an argument to use MULTICAST instead of OBSERVER everywhere.

The main counterargument is that OBSERVER works just fine for simple systems, and lots of systems are built successfully from it.

Clearly Ralph believes OBSERVER and MULTICAST are distinct, related, and dependent in some sense. Aha! thought I, isn't there a similar relationship between ABSTRACT FACTORY and FACTORY METHOD? ABSTRACT FACTORY uses FACTORY METHOD, and yet these are separate patterns. But he demurs:

There are lots of ways for patterns to depend on each other. It is possible to make an abstract factory that does not use FACTORY METHOD, but I claim that it isn't possible to have a multicast that does not use OBSERVER. I'd be happy to be proven wrong.

Well, I can imagine applying MULTICAST to implement a many-to-one dependency, which is the opposite of OBSERVER's stated intent (a one-to-many dependency). We've never duked this one out, but I predict he would claim that this too is an example of OBSERVER. A many-to-one dependency can be viewed as multiple degenerate applications of the pattern; that is, many-to-one is just a collection of subject–observer pairs all sharing the same observer. Voilà!

Phooey, I say.

There's another way around my counterexample, which is to claim that OBSERVER's intent is just plain wrong—that one-to-many isn't a valid constraint on OBSERVER. Well of course. We can prove anything we want about a pattern if we can change it. Not that I think our patterns are sacrosanct or anything; I simply prefer to change only one variable at a time, and at present that variable is called "MULTICAST," not "OBSERVER."

Which brings us to a whole 'nother can of worms—that of MULTICAST's intent.

Intent

Deliver information to interested objects at arbitrary times through an extensible interface.

Erich and I thought this summed up the pattern's intent rather well. Ralph, however, thinks it says virtually nothing. He argues that there should be no difference in intent between MULTICAST and OBSERVER, which is perhaps the best argument for making them one and the same pattern.

> I claim that MULTICAST and OBSERVER are used for the *exact same purpose*. In other words, they have the same intent. I think that the current Intent for MULTICAST is misleading because it hides this fact. On the other hand, FACTORY METHOD and ABSTRACT FACTORY have different intents.
>
> In my opinion, MULTICAST is a special case of OBSERVER, a more complicated case. This is not a proof that there shouldn't be two patterns in the catalog, just something to consider when you are deciding what *should* be there.

Ralph's comments sum up one side of the controversy that surrounded MULTICAST. The opposing viewpoint maintains that MULTICAST and OBSERVER are indeed related, but that they're different enough to warrant independent treatments. The battle lines demarcate typing philosophies too, with proponents of weakly typed languages on one side and those favoring strong typing on the other. Strong-typers prefer to make MULTICAST its own pattern; weak-typers think it's a logical extension of OBSERVER. Among the Gang of Four, Ralph is the lone weak-typer.

The waning arguments for an independent MULTICAST came from Richard:

> I still believe that OBSERVER/MULTICAST are different but related patterns. . . . Think about what concepts are varying: In OBSERVER, it really is the concrete observers, and possibly the aspects[2] of the subjects. In MULTICAST, it is the types of events. To me this is the key difference between the two patterns. I do not see MULTICAST as an extension to OBSERVER or vice versa for this reason. . . .
>
> Note that in common to both patterns there is the *solution* concept of registration and notification. But this is basically a mechanism to allow senders and receivers to be bound at run-time. It is not intrinsic to the *problem* each pattern is solving but to the fact that these patterns establish relationships between objects, and registration/notification is a basic mechanism (pattern?) to do this.
>
> [Think also about] scope and variations. In this light, I think that the variations to MULTICAST include:
>
> 1. M_a: Global notification, registering with the Event class; for example, `MyEvent::register(MyEventHandler)`—"broadcast" as per John's [example].
> 2. M_b: Local notification, registering with the sender; for example, `Sender::registerMyEventHandler(MyEventHandler)`—per Erich's preference and closer to my idea of "narrowcast."
> 3. M_c: Local notification, registering with the sender and using a single Event class; for example, `Event`.
>
> Similarly, variations on OBSERVER include:
>
> 1. O_a: Notification of nonspecific change (naive OBSERVER); for example, `Observer::update()`.
> 2. O_b: Notification of semispecific change; for example, hints—`Subject::register(Aspect, Observer)`.
> 3. O_c: Notification of specific change; for example, an event—`Subject::registerMyEvent(MyEventHandler)`.
>
> Note that M_b and O_c are very similar, as are O_a and M_c.
>
> In this perspective, (a) OBSERVER is a refinement of MULTICAST, but equally, (b) MULTICAST is a refinement of OBSERVER. It is just that with

---

2. An *aspect* is an object that specifies the change precisely. Supplying an aspect along with the notification can make updating much easier for the observer. *Design Patterns* mentions aspects in item 7 on page 298.

(a) you have limited the scope of events more and more to arrive at a specialized OBSERVER. With (b) you have extended the scope of Subject changes in OBSERVER to arrive at a specialized MULTICAST. Both views are valid.

Exactly the same phenomenon [occurs] when you push traversals into the Visitor, [producing something] close to ITERATOR. Or you extend STRATEGY to arrive at BUILDER.

I always like to start with the naive patterns and see what kinds of changes you have to make to arrive at another pattern. From the preceding, you have to go from M_a to M_b to M_c to O_a to get from MULTICAST to OBSERVER. I have always maintained that wisdom about patterns comes from the space between them.

Erudite as this is, Ralph took issue with almost all of it. The details aren't important; let's just say we were at an impasse. When our discussions reach such a quasimathematical level, I know the end is near, one way or the other. And I was right: An amicable resolution was just around the corner—but I'm getting ahead of myself.

Beyond the specter of never reaching closure, what worried me most about this debate was the small sample set of opinions. So I was delighted when Bob Martin volunteered these thoughts to me [Martin97], even before he uttered them, because I know how firmly ensconced he is on the strong typing side:

I wanted to respond to the issue you raised in [the MULTICAST discussion]. Is MULTICAST just a variation on OBSERVER? I think not. And the reason that I think not is that observers know their subjects. But MULTICAST handlers don't have to know their event sources.

In OBSERVER, you want to know when the state of something changes. So you register an observer on that thing. But in MULTICAST you are interested in the occurrence of a particular event. You don't care about the source of that event. (Which, by the way, is why I liked your idea about putting the registration function in the Event rather than Erich's notion of putting the registration interface on the event source.)[3]

Consider a keyboard event. We may have a system with a keyboard and a keypad. Both these devices produce keyboard events. The software doesn't care about the source. It doesn't care whether the "3" key

---

3. Just to make Erich's position clear, he isn't opposed to putting the registration interface in the Event class. He simply wants the Motivation's exposition to reflect the general case that's described in subsequent sections.

was hit on the keypad or on the keyboard; it just wants to know which keys were hit. We could make the same argument using a mouse and a joystick, or anything where there might be multiple event sources.

I think this is a fundamental difference between MULTICAST and OBSERVER. In MULTICAST we are still observing something, but we don't know what we are observing. The thing we register with is not the thing that generates the stimuli that we are interested in.

The keyboard-versus-keypad example is particularly germane. It reinforces a point I made earlier when I compared the relationship between MULTICAST and OBSERVER to that of ABSTRACT FACTORY and FACTORY METHOD (page 134). The most common implementation of ABSTRACT FACTORY uses a factory method for each product, but that doesn't mean we make ABSTRACT FACTORY an extension of FACTORY METHOD. They are different patterns because they have fundamentally different intents.

Similarly, viewing MULTICAST as an extension of OBSERVER runs counter to their respective purposes. OBSERVER maintains a one-to-many dependency between objects, while MULTICAST is about delivering encapsulated information to objects in a type-safe and yet extensible fashion. To underscore the difference, I posited using MULTICAST to implement a many-to-one dependency—exactly Bob's example and clearly outside OBSERVER's intent.

Q.E.D., or so I thought. Leave it to Erich to snatch defeat from the jaws of victory.

In my Design Patterns and Java course, I had to explain the new JDK 1.1 event-handling model. So it all came back to me again. It turns out in explaining the design that it was really easy to [introduce] this as an OBSERVER relationship, since everybody was familiar with that. In the next step, I explained the refinements on typed events and registering interests. So I think it is important to state that MULTICAST is a refinement of OBSERVER and [to describe] what it refines instead of arguing whether MULTICAST is different from OBSERVER. This doesn't answer the question of whether a refinement deserves its own pattern. I still think it does.

Actually, there is another example of this in GoF. At some point we argued whether BUILDER isn't just a Strategy for creating things. Obviously BUILDER made it into the book as a separate pattern.

Regarding the name: After reading the arguments about types, I'm getting attracted by the name "typed message."

One might say Erich was speaking heresy, the assertion at the end of his first paragraph notwithstanding. It was, in retrospect, the last gasp of MULTICAST as we knew it.

I for one was taken aback—but in a good way. Things finally seemed to be clicking. But like any prudent soul contemplating a one-eighty, and ever the bottom-liner, I wanted to make sure I understood the implications of this epiphany:

> So you're advocating stripping registration and delivery out of MULTICAST, putting it into OBSERVER, and saving the rest for TYPED MESSAGE?

The reply was exceptionally quick.

> Yes, I think this is it. Remember that we already discuss the registration for interests in OBSERVER (see *Design Patterns*, page 298, bullet 7). The more I think about it, the more I like it. . . .

Lest the import be lost on you, mellow, even-tempered Erich is expressing excitement here—a propitious sign.

Ralph gave his blessing shortly thereafter:

> I would be a lot happier with MULTICAST/TYPED MESSAGE if it were presented the way Erich said. The relationship to OBSERVER is so obvious that when we don't emphasize it, it makes me think we are trying to hide something.
>
> When we wrote our book, we *were* trying to hide something. We were trying to avoid talking about one pattern being a specialization of another, or one pattern containing another as a component. We wanted to avoid going meta and just wanted to talk about patterns. This was part of why we didn't describe "abstract class" as a pattern, since most of the patterns would have contained it.
>
> I think that was a good decision for the first patterns catalog, but the world is different now. People want to know the relationship between patterns and we need to tell them. The relationship here is so obvious that we need to emphasize it, not just tuck it away at the end in the Related Patterns section.

Well now, those long-standing battle lines suddenly seem quaint and irrelevant. We would extend OBSERVER only as necessary to account for a new pattern, TYPED MESSAGE. The synergy between the two would render a separate MULTICAST pattern redundant.

What does this new pattern look like? Quite similar to MULTICAST, actually—at least as of this writing. We are admittedly a long way from a polished TYPED MESSAGE. In the meantime, here is a sketch of the current strawman.

Intent

Encapsulate information in an object to allow its type-safe transmission. Clients may extend the object to add information without compromising type safety.

Motivation

[Basically the vending machine example from MULTICAST with minor changes to emphasize the encapsulation and extension of events and to de-emphasize the notification process. Some of the more detailed code has been moved to the Sample Code section.]

Applicability

Use TYPED MESSAGE when *all* of the following are true:

- Certain classes of objects may be interested in receiving information from other objects.
- The information is of arbitrary structure and complexity and may vary as the software evolves.
- The information transfer should be statically type-safe.

[Exactly the same as MULTICAST's.]

Structure

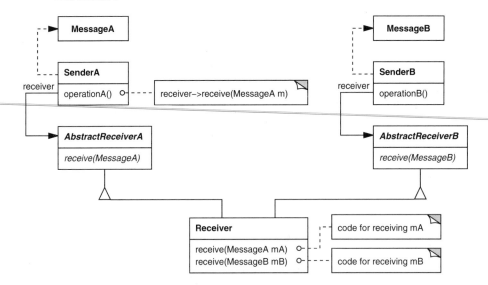

Participants

Message (ProductDispensedEvent)

- encapsulates information to be transferred from Sender to Receiver.

Sender (Dispenser)

- maintains a reference to a Receiver object.
- implements one or more operations that involve sending a message to the receiver.

AbstractReceiver (ProductDispensedHandler)

- defines an interface for receiving a Message object.

Receiver (CoinChanger)

- implements one or more AbstractReceiver interfaces.

Collaborations

- A sender instantiates a message and delivers it to its receiver.
- A message is passive—it does not initiate communication with senders or receivers.

Consequences

1. Information can be passed type-safely and extensibly without downcasts or switch statements . . .
2. Supports implicit invocation when combined with OBSERVER . . .
3. Lack of multiple (interface) inheritance makes application difficult . . .
4. May lead to convoluted inheritance graphs . . .

Implementation

1. There needn't be a one-to-one relationship between Message classes and AbstractReceiver interfaces . . .
2. Lumping Message and Sender improves extensibility but makes it harder to tell who sends a given Message . . .

3. Implementing TYPED MESSAGE in a weakly typed language or one lacking multiple inheritance . . .

4. Combining TYPED MESSAGE and OBSERVER . . .

5. Trade-offs in defining a common base class for Messages . . .

Sample Code

[Code snippets lifted from the Motivation's vending machine example. Includes variant implementations such as the lumped Sender-Message design described earlier (page 130) and an implementation using composition instead of multiple inheritance.]

Known Uses

Java's JDK 1.1 [Java97] uses TYPED MESSAGE in conjunction with OBSERVER in its "delegation-based event model," as Erich mentioned. I have used it in at least one project at IBM Research, but that work is as yet unpublished. As always, other known uses are most welcome!

Related Patterns

[OBSERVER is related, of course, but that will have been made abundantly clear by the time you get to this section.]

Typed messages may be mistaken for commands (see COMMAND [GoF95]). Here again, the difference has to do with intent. A command encapsulates an operation, whereas a typed message encapsulates state. One is active, the other is passive. TYPED MESSAGE also has an emphasis on type-safe extension that COMMAND lacks.

TYPED MESSAGE may seem closer to a pattern that's often used with COMMAND, namely MEMENTO. But MEMENTO's intent is the opposite of TYPED MESSAGE's: A memento must *avoid* transferring information to other objects. The information it encapsulates is for its originator's eyes only.

Talk about coincidences. At about the time we settled on TYPED MESSAGE, Paul Pelletier was (unknowingly) applying Cope's curiously recurring template pattern [Coplien95] to MULTICAST and (unknowingly) wound up with a streamlined way to implement our new pattern [Pelletier97].

After reading [about your MULTICAST-based design] I thought, "Hey, a nice template could probably be created to simplify even more the creation of new events. . . ." After playing with this idea for a while, I came up with the following code. The part I'm not too sure about is the way the template is used, using the derived class we're creating as an argument:

```
class CoinInsertedEvent : public TEvent<CoinInsertedEvent>
```

I've never seen templates used this way, but I can see now that this could be a useful way to have the type checking done at compile-time. Does this way of using a template have a special name?

Another nice thing about using the template is that the Handler interface is automatically generated as part of the TEvent class itself, simplifying even more the addition of new events:

```
#include <iostream.h>
#include <stdio.h>
#include <list>

using namespace std;

template <class T>
class TEvent {
public:
    class Handler {
    public:
        Handler () { TEvent<T>::register(this); }
        virtual int handleEvent(const T& t) = 0;
    };

    typedef list<Handler*> HandlerList;

    static void register (Handler* aHandler) {
        registry.push_back(aHandler);
    }

    static void notify (TEvent<T>* t) {
        HandlerList::iterator i;
        for (
            i = registry.begin(); i != registry.end(); i++
        ) {
            (*i)->handleEvent(*(T*) t);
        }
    }

    void Notify () { T::notify(this); }
```

```
    private:
        static HandlerList registry;
    };
    class CoinInsertedEvent :
        public TEvent<CoinInsertedEvent> { };
    class CoinReleaseEvent :
        public TEvent<CoinReleaseEvent> { };
    class ProductDispensedEvent :
        public TEvent<ProductDispensedEvent> { };

    class CoinChanger :
        public CoinReleaseEvent::Handler,
        public ProductDispensedEvent::Handler {
    public:
        int handleEvent (const ProductDispensedEvent& event) {
            cout << "Changer::Coin dispensed." << endl;
            return 0;
        }
        int handleEvent (const CoinReleaseEvent& event) {
            cout << "Changer::Coin released." << endl;
            return 0;
        }
    };

    TEvent<CoinInsertedEvent>::HandlerList
        TEvent<CoinInsertedEvent>::registry;
    TEvent<CoinReleaseEvent>::HandlerList
        TEvent<CoinReleaseEvent>::registry;
    TEvent<ProductDispensedEvent>::HandlerList
        TEvent<ProductDispensedEvent>::registry;

    int main (int, char**) {
        CoinReleaseEvent coinReleaseEvent;
        CoinChanger coinChanger;
        ProductDispensedEvent productDispensedEvent;

        coinReleaseEvent.Notify();
        productDispensedEvent.Notify();
    }
```

Note that TYPED MESSAGE comprises all but the registration and notification machinery of this implementation. (Hmm, more fodder for the Implementation and Sample Code sections. Bravo, Paul!)

CHAPTER 5

Seven Habits of Effective Pattern Writers

I f you think object-oriented development is hard to do well, try *pattern* development! The mathematician in me likes to think of it as the "integration" of object-oriented design: It's the sum of innumerable little experiences over an interval of applications. Yet pattern development seems a good deal harder than what I learned in calculus class. Integrals don't interfere with one another, which lets you solve them independently (although knowing how to solve one often helps you solve others). A pattern, in contrast, doesn't work in a vacuum. It provides the solution to just one problem, so it must cooperate with other patterns. Hence a pattern writer must contemplate not one pattern but several, even some as yet unwritten—and that's but one of many challenges in the pattern development process. If you're an aspiring pattern writer, you'll need all the help you can get.

We certainly learned a lot about pattern development while writing *Design Patterns*. And we're still learning, as you may have gathered from the last chapter. What I've tried to do in this closing chapter is boil our experience down to seven habits we've adopted, largely unconsciously, over many years of writing patterns. Taking these habits to heart should help you hone your pattern-writing abilities far faster than we did.

Habit 1: Taking Time to Reflect

The single most important activity in pattern writing is *reflection*. Bruce Anderson, an early influence on our work, has offered up this mantra for years. Take time off periodically to reflect on what you've done. Think about the systems you've built, the problems you've had, and how you solved (or didn't solve) them.

Such diversions are all but unthinkable in this day of ever-shortening development times. But reflection is crucial. There's no better way to get into a creative rut than to hack mindlessly. You may produce lots of working code, but code mass is a poor measure of one's productivity. The mark of a good design is precisely the opposite—it is small and elegant. It does much without bulk. It implements everything "once and only once," as Kent Beck likes to say. It's also flexible; large bodies of code generally aren't.

Now, it's probably impractical to expect people to take a month off per year for contemplation. But what you *can* do is record your experiences *incrementally*. When you have a nontrivial problem to solve, try to write about it immediately. Jot down some notes describing the problem and why it's difficult. Then start working on it. Whenever you try a new approach, jot it down. If it fails, jot that down too, along with *why* it failed. Do the same if it succeeds. Almost everyone can spend five percent of their time jotting down experience—it just takes discipline.

If you do this religiously, you'll be amazed at the written experience you accumulate. This is the raw material of patterns. There's still much to do, certainly, but you've got the all-important nuggets of wisdom from which to refine the gold.

Another important activity along these lines is to look at as many other systems as you can, systems designed by other people. The best way to learn from other systems is to actually build with them. If you don't have the time or money to do that, then at least read about them. Seek an understanding of the problems they address and how they address them. Study specifications and documentation. Read papers on research systems. Browse through *OOPSLA* and *ECOOP* proceedings. *Software—Practice & Experience* is another good source of design and implementation information.

When you examine a system, glean everything you can from it. Try to identify patterns you already know. Evaluate how the solutions you find vary from those of published patterns. Be on the lookout for novel design solutions—they may represent new patterns. But keep in mind that relatively few design solutions are truly new. More often, people use variations on known solutions. A new and/or unique solution might not be widely applicable enough to cast in pattern form.

If you do find something that seems new, make sure it is applicable in other contexts before you try to write it up as a pattern. The GoF had one inviolable rule as we developed *Design Patterns*: We had to find *two* existing examples of a problem and its solution before we would write a pattern for it. This was a particularly important rule for us to follow; we were exploring unfamiliar territory, and we wanted to make sure what we wrote was grounded in reality—we didn't want to end up with a set of solutions to problems no one had. Ultimately, we discarded many patterns that seemed quite appealing and potentially useful but hadn't seen real use.

Habit 2: Adhering to a Structure

Once you have the raw materials, how do you go about writing them up in pattern form?

Well, first of all, don't assume there is only *one* pattern form. No one form suits everybody. Some people prefer a more prosey style like Alexander's. Others favor the more fine-grained approach used in *Design Patterns*. Still others adopt totally different structures. The attribute shared by all these structures is just that—*structure*.

If there's one catchphrase that people largely agree on, it is the Alexandrian canon that a pattern is "a solution to a problem in a context." Now I'll be so bold as to amend the canon: A pattern is a *structured exposition of* a solution to a problem in a context. Patterns have recognizable parts that guide their application and comparison. These parts include a name, a statement of the problem, the context and justification of its solution, and the solution itself. This is essentially the structure of Alexander's patterns. Our patterns further decompose these fundamental elements into more focused treatments, such as the Applicability, Participants, and Consequences sections. The proceedings of the

Pattern Languages of Programs (PLoP) conferences [CS95, MRB98, VCK96] include surprisingly diverse variations on these themes.

So the first step in getting a pattern down on paper is to decide on its structure. The more information your average pattern has, the more important the structure becomes. Consistent structure lends uniformity to patterns, letting people compare them easily. Structure also helps people search for information. Less structure means more prose, which might be fine for casual reading but unacceptable for comparison and reference purposes.

Once you've settled on a structure, make sure you follow it consistently. You needn't be afraid to change the structure, but you'll have to change it in every pattern—and that gets increasingly expensive as your patterns mature.

Habit 3: Being Concrete Early and Often

In our patterns, the Motivation section comes up front. That's because people seem to understand concepts better when they are presented in concrete terms first and then in more abstract terms. The concrete example in the Motivation section gives the reader a frame of reference for the problem and its solution. Another thing that section demonstrates is why other approaches to the problem fail, again in concrete terms. With the Motivation section as an introduction, the reader is better able to appreciate the general solution.

A corollary to concreteness is the need for lots of examples from the real world. Examples should *not* be the sole estate of a Motivation section. Use examples and counterexamples throughout the pattern to illustrate key points. Even the most abstract sections in our template (i.e., Applicability, Structure, Participants, and Collaborations) at times include examples. For instance, some Collaborations sections include interaction diagrams that show how objects communicate at run-time. Refer to such examples when discussing the abstract aspects of the pattern—be concrete even when you're being abstract.

Another corollary might be termed "telling the whole truth." That means you must warn your reader about the potential pitfalls of the pattern. It's all too easy to dwell on its positive aspects; it's not so easy to appreciate a pattern's faults and talk frankly about them. No pattern is free of drawbacks, be it extra cost, ill-behavior under certain circumstances, or whatever. Make sure your reader understands how the pattern can fall short.

Habit 4: Keeping Patterns Distinct and Complementary

There's a tendency to avoid when you're developing multiple patterns. As you work on a pattern, it tends to grow both in detail and in scope. It's easy to forget about other patterns in the meantime. The distinctions between patterns blur as a result, making it hard for others to understand the patterns collectively. They start to overlap in scope and purpose. All this may seem perfectly clear to the author, but it probably won't be clear to newcomers. They won't know when to use one pattern and not another, because their differences aren't obvious.

Therefore make sure your patterns are orthogonal and that they work synergistically. Continually ask yourself, "How is pattern *X* different from pattern *Y*?" If two patterns solve the same or similar problems, you can probably merge them. Don't worry if two patterns employ similar class hierarchies. There are only so many ways to use the relatively few mechanisms inherent in object-oriented programming. Often the same arrangement of classes will yield substantially different object structures that address widely varying problems. Let the *intents* of the patterns be your guide to their differences and not the class structures that implement them.

A good way to promote orthogonality and synergy in your patterns is by keeping separate documents that compare and contrast them. In *Design Patterns* we dedicated several sections to this purpose. The simple act of trying to explain pattern relationships in written form gave us new perspectives on our patterns. More than once it forced us to rethink some of them.

My only regret is that we didn't concentrate on relationships earlier in the game. I recommend you start writing down such supplementary material as soon as possible. It may seem like a silly thing to do, especially when you don't have a lot of patterns to compare; but as soon as you have just two patterns, the possibility of overlap emerges. Spending time comparing and contrasting them early on will help you keep your patterns distinct and complementary.

Habit 5: Presenting Effectively

The quality of your patterns is determined by how well you present them. You could discover the best pattern in the world, but it won't help anyone unless you convey it effectively.

By "presenting" I mean two things: typesetting and writing style. Good typesetting is a matter of skill in page layout, typography, and graphics, not to mention printer quality. Use the best software tools (word processor, drawing editor, and so on) you can. Make liberal use of drawings to illustrate key points. You may not think you need any drawings, but chances are you do. At the very least, they break monotony, and at best drawings will get your point across as no amount of explanation can. Not all drawings have to be formal class and object diagrams; often, informal drawings or even sketches convey just as much information and sometimes more. If you are "artistically challenged," have someone else do the drawings for you.

Good writing style is even more important than good typesetting. Write clearly and unpretentiously. Favor a down-to-earth style rather than a stuffy, academic one. People understand and appreciate a conversational tone, making them more receptive to the material. Clarity and ease of reading are important in most writing, but they're especially important for pattern writing. The pattern concept is new enough and the subject matter complicated enough that some people have a hard time seeing the point of it all. Do everything you can to make a pattern approachable.

The best way to learn how to write conversationally is to try your hand at it. Make sure everything you write is something you could hear yourself saying to friend. Avoid the passive voice. Break up long sentences and paragraphs. Use everyday words, and don't be afraid to use contractions. Above all, make it sound natural.

Another thing everyone should do at some point in life is read a book or two on writing style. There are many to choose from. My three favorites are Strunk and White's *The Elements of Style* [SW79] (its organization, remarkably, is not unlike a series of patterns), Joseph M. Williams' *Style: Ten Lessons in Clarity and Grace* [Williams85], and John R. Trimble's *Writing with Style: Conversations on the Art of Writing* [Trimble75]. Books like these are packed with tips and techniques for good, clear writing. They can help you improve your patterns independent of their technical content.

Habit 6: Iterating Tirelessly

You won't get a pattern right the first time. You won't even get it right the first ten times. In fact, you'll probably never get it totally right. Pattern writing is an ongoing process. The fact that the field is new doesn't help matters. But even if it weren't . . . even if there were lots of examples of good patterns and books to help you write them, pattern development (like any other kind of development) would still be an iterative process.

Expect to write and rewrite your patterns many times. Don't look for perfection in one pattern before you begin work on the next. Remember, patterns don't exist in isolation; they affect one another. A significant change to one could very well impact others. As with any iteration, your efforts should converge at some point, but that's just the point at which the patterns have stabilized enough to let other people read, understand, and comment on them.

Habit 7: Collecting and Incorporating Feedback

Cervantes was right: "The proof of the pudding is in the eating." The acid test of a pattern comes when it's put to use. Actually, no pattern can be trusted until it is used by *someone other than its author.* Patterns have this insidious habit of being perfectly understandable to people who are familiar with the problem involved and its solution. Such people have used the pattern before unconsciously. When they see the pattern, they can recognize it immediately, even if it isn't presented very well. The real challenge is to make the pattern understandable to people who have never run across the problem before. There's no way to do that without getting and incorporating feedback from just such people.

Encourage your colleagues to discuss design in terms of your patterns, and be available to participate in such discussions. Look for opportunities to use the patterns in your day-to-day work. Try to disseminate your patterns as widely as you can. You might even submit them to conferences like PLoP or to publications like *C++ Report, Smalltalk Report, Java Report,* and *Journal of Object-Oriented Programming*. Such exposure should yield lots of good feedback.

Once comments start rolling in, be prepared to hear the worst. I can't remember how many times I was shocked to learn that something thoroughly comprehensible to me thoroughly confounded someone else. The negative feedback can be disheartening, especially at the beginning when you're most vulnerable and also most likely to get it. Even though some criticism might not be valid or might result from a simple misunderstanding, most of it will probably be legitimate. Give your reviewers the benefit of the doubt. Bend over backwards to make them happy. You may end up making many, many more people happy in the long run.

No Silver Bullet

Adopting these habits won't guarantee your success as a pattern writer, you understand. Nor is this list exhaustive—Meszaros and Doble in particular go several steps further [MD98]. But it should at least help you focus your efforts profitably. The better your patterns are, the more impact they'll have.

That's not to say everyone should be off writing patterns. Pattern writing involves a nontrivial investment of time and effort, and not everyone can justify it. I encourage everyone to try writing a pattern or two, because you can't know whether you're good at it otherwise. As time goes on, however, I expect the number of pattern *writers* to be dwarfed by the number of pattern *users*—much as programming language users (thankfully) dwarf the ranks of language creators.

Bibliography

[AIS+77] Alexander, C., S. Ishikawa, M. Silverstein, et al. *A Pattern Language*. Oxford University Press, New York, 1977.

[ASC96] Accredited Standards Committee. Working paper for draft proposed international standard for information systems—programming language C++. Doc. No. X3J16/96–0225, WG21/N1043, December 2, 1996.

[Betz97] Betz, M. E-mail communication, May 27, 1997.

[Burchall95] Burchall, L. E-mail communication, June 21, 1995.

[BCC+96] Beck, K., J.O. Coplien, R. Crocker, et al. Industrial experience with design patterns. *Proceedings of the 18th International Conference on Software Engineering* (pp. 103–114), Berlin, Germany, March 1996.

[BFV+96] Budinsky, F., M. Finnie, J. Vlissides, et al. Automatic code generation from design patterns. *IBM Systems Journal*, 35(2):151–171, 1996. *http://www.almaden.ibm.com/journal/sj/budin/budinsky.html*.

[BMR+96] Buschmann, F., R. Meunier, H. Rohnert, et al. *Pattern-Oriented Software Architecture—A System of Patterns*. Wiley and Sons Ltd., Chichester, England, 1996.

[Coplien92] Coplien, J. *Advanced C++ Programming Styles and Idioms.* Addison-Wesley, Reading, MA, 1992.

[Coplien95] Coplien, J. Curiously recurring template patterns. *C++ Report,* 7(2):40–43, 1995.

[Coplien96] Coplien, J. *Software Patterns.* SIGS Books, New York, 1996.

[CS95] Coplien, J., and D. Schmidt (Eds.). *Pattern Languages of Program Design.* Addison-Wesley, Reading, MA, 1995.

[CZ96] Clark, C., and B. Zino. E-mail communication, October 28, 1996.

[Forté97] Forté Software, Inc. *Customizing Forté Express Applications.* Oakland, CA, 1997.

[Fowler97] Fowler, M. *Analysis Patterns: Reusable Object Models.* Addison-Wesley, Reading, MA, 1997.

[Gabriel95] Gabriel, R. E-mail communication, April 14, 1995.

[Gamma91] Gamma, E. *Object-Oriented Software Development Based on ET++: Design Patterns, Class Library, Tools* (in German). PhD thesis, University of Zurich, Institut für Informatik, 1991.

[Gamma95] Gamma, E. E-mail communication, March 8, 1995.

[GoF95] Gamma, E., R. Helm, R. Johnson, et al. *Design Patterns: Elements of Reusable Object-Oriented Software.* Addison-Wesley, Reading, MA, 1995.

[Hay96] Hay, D. *Data Model Patterns: Conventions of Thought.* Dorset House, New York, 1996.

[Henney96] Henney, K. E-mail communication, September 15, 1996.

[HJE95] Hüni, H., R. Johnson, and R. Engel. A framework for network protocol software. *OOPSLA '95 Conference Proceedings* (published as ACM *SIGPLAN Notices*), 30(10):358–369, 1995.

[Java97] JavaSoft, Inc. *Java Development Kit Version 1.1.* Mountain View, CA, 1997.

[Kotula96] Kotula, J. Discovering patterns: An industry report. *Software—Practice & Experience,* 26(11):1261–1276, 1996.

[KP88] Krasner, G., and S. Pope. A cookbook for using the Model-View-Controller user interface paradigm in Smalltalk-80. *Journal of Object-Oriented Programming*, 1(3):26–49, 1988.

[LVC89] Linton, M., J. Vlissides, and P. Calder. Composing user interfaces with InterViews. *Computer*, 22(2):8–22, 1989.

[Martin97] Martin, R. E-mail communication, July 24, 1997.

[McCosker97] McCosker, M. E-mail communication, March 4, 1997.

[Meyers95] Meyers, S. E-mail communication, January 31, 1995.

[MD98] Meszaros, G., and J. Doble. A pattern language for pattern writing. In [MRB98].

[MRB98] Martin, R., D. Riehle, and F. Buschmann (Eds.). *Pattern Languages of Program Design 3*. Addison-Wesley, Reading, MA, 1998.

[Pelletier97] Pelletier, P. E-mail communication, June 22, 1997.

[Peierls96] Peierls, T. E-mail communication, February 16, 1996.

[Prechelt97] Prechelt, L. An experiment on the usefulness of design patterns: Detailed description and evaluation. Technical Report 9/1997, University of Karlsruhe, Germany, June 1997.

[PUS97] Prechelt, L., B. Unger, and D.C. Schmidt. Replication of the first controlled experiment on the usefulness of design patterns: Detailed description and evaluation. Technical Report WUCS–97–34, Washington University, Department of Computer Science, St. Louis, December 1997.

[PD96] *patterns-discussion@cs.uiuc.edu*, December 12, 1996.

[Schmid95] Schmid, H. Creating the architecture of a manufacturing framework by design patterns. *OOPSLA '95 Conference Proceedings* (published as ACM *SIGPLAN Notices*), 30(10):370–384, 1995.

[Schmidt96a] Schmidt, D. E-mail communication, January 2, 1996.

[Schmidt96b] Schmidt, D. E-mail communication, January 9, 1996.

[Schmidt96c] Schmidt, D. E-mail communication, February 7, 1996.

[Schmidt96d] Schmidt, D. E-mail communication, February 8, 1996.

[Siegel96] Siegel, J. *CORBA Fundamentals and Programming*. Wiley, New York, 1996.

[SH98] Schmidt, D., and T. Harrison. Double-checked locking. In [MRB98].

[SV97] Schmidt, D., and S. Vinoski. The OMG event object service. *C++ Report*, 9(2):37–46, 52, 1997.

[SW79] Strunk, W., and E.B. White. *The Elements of Style* (3rd ed.). Macmillan, New York, 1979.

[Trimble75] Trimble, J. *Writing with Style: Conversations on the Art of Writing*. Prentice-Hall, Englewood Cliffs, NJ, 1975.

[VanCamp96] Van Camp, D. E-mail communication, September 23, 1996.

[Vlissides96] Vlissides, J. Generation gap. *C++ Report*, 8(10):12–18, 1996.

[VCK96] Vlissides, J., J. Coplien, and N. Kerth (Eds.). *Pattern Languages of Program Design 2*. Addison-Wesley, Reading, MA, 1996.

[VT91] Vlissides, J., and S. Tang. A Unidraw-based user interface builder. *Proceedings of the ACM SIGGRAPH Fourth Annual Symposium on User Interface Software and Technology* (pp. 201–210). Hilton Head, SC, November 1991.

[Wendland97] Wendland, G. E-mail communication, January 10, 1997.

[Williams85] Williams, J. *Style: Ten Lessons in Clarity and Grace* (2nd ed.). Scott, Foresman and Co., Glenview, IL, 1985.

Index

A

abstract class
   declaring in C++; 113–114
ABSTRACT FACTORY
   See also [GoF95], pp. 87–95
   FACTORY METHOD and; 134–135, 138
   instance ownership, contrast with
      SINGLETON; 62
   pattern sections
      intent, compared with FACTORY
         METHOD's; 135, 138
      intent, compared with other creational
         patterns; 48
AbstractReceiver participant
   of MULTICAST; 129–130
   of TYPED MESSAGE; 140–141
access
   control
      database advantages over file
         systems; 96
      issues for Singleton destructor design; 62
   privileges, *See* protection
ADAPTER
   See also [GoF95], pp. 139–150
   design aspects that can be varied with; 25
adoption
   creation contrasted with; 19
   orphan relationship to; 22–24

Alexander, Christopher
   definition of a pattern; 3
      amended; 147
   pattern development as discovery
         process; ix
   pattern-writing style; 8
   quality without a name; 5
aliases
   See symbolic links
Anderson, Bruce
   as early influence on GoF; 146
annotation for patterns
   Gamma style; 58–59
   Vlissides style; 29
applicability
   See also design patterns, pattern sections
   Applicability section
      as extension of Alexander's pattern
         form; 147
      importance of concrete examples in; 148
   COMPOSITE; 16, 54
   GENERATION GAP; 92
   MULTICAST; 131
   PROXY; 26
   in several contexts, importance for pattern
         development; 147
   TEMPLATE METHOD; 42
   TYPED MESSAGE; 140

157

Related Patterns Resources

Capturing a wealth of experience about the design of object-oriented software, four top-notch designers present a catalog of simple and succinct solutions to commonly occurring design problems. Previously undocumented, these 23 patterns allow designers to create more flexible, elegant, and ultimately reusable designs without having to rediscover the design solutions themselves.

0-201-63361-2

Use the contents of the *Design Patterns* book to create your own design documents and reusable components. The CD contains:

- 23 patterns to cut & paste into your design documents
- Sample code demonstrating pattern implementation
- Complete *Design Patterns* content in standard HTML format, with numerous hyper-linked cross-references
- Access through a standard web browser
- Java-based dynamic search mechanism

0-201-63498-8

Also available from Addison-Wesley:

Software Patterns Series http://www2.awl.com/cseng/sps/index.html